Paul Coleman Cochran
G.T.S.
new York
1970

Robert C. Dentan

PREFACE TO
OLD TESTAMENT
THEOLOGY

REVISED EDITION

New York  1963

Copyright, 1950, by Yale University Press
Copyright © 1963 by Robert C. Dentan
Library of Congress Catalog Card Number: 63-16290
426-863-C-3.5
Printed in the United States of America

To My Wife

PREFACE TO THE REVISED EDITION

In view of the flood of works on Old Testament theology and related subjects that has poured from the press since 1949, the appearance of a revised edition of this little book hardly needs justification. Teachers and students have kindly testified to its usefulness for preliminary orientation in the field, but this usefulness has been increasingly diminished by the obsolescence of the historical survey and bibliography. In the present revision I have brought the historical section up to date, and amplified the bibliography by a section devoted to works published between 1949 and 1963. The size of this section is the best indication of the importance the subject has acquired in recent years.

It would have expanded the study far beyond the modest limits envisioned for it if I had also attempted to enter into extensive dialogue with those who have discussed the nature and method of Old Testament theology since 1949; Part II, therefore, remains substantially unchanged. I like to think that, at the least, it has considerable heuristic value. But I must also confess—perhaps to my shame—that my views have not altered in any essential respect as a result of more recent discussion. The method of presenting the subject defended here still seems to me to provide a broader framework for presenting the *whole* religion of the Old Testament and to be more useful to the student of Christian theology than any of the alternatives offered. The one particular in which I might be inclined to modify my position would be in laying greater stress upon the necessity of showing that revelation in Israel was historical revelation. But I suspect this result can be better achieved within the framework here suggested than by the substitution of any radically new scheme; the fact that the God of Israel was known through his activity in historical events is, after all, only a single aspect—though admittedly a very basic one—of the Old Testament doctrine of God.

R. C. D.

General Theological Seminary
March 18, 1963

PREFACE

There has been much discussion of Old Testament theology in recent years, but no systematic study of its history, nature and method has been made since Oehler published his *Prolegomena zur Theologie des Alten Testaments* a little over a hundred years ago. It seemed worth while in view of contemporary interest in the subject to undertake that task once again. The following essay is an attempt to define Old Testament theology in such a way as to do justice both to the experience of the past as reflected in the history of the discipline and also to the special needs of the contemporary theological world. As I have had in mind chiefly the requirements of the theological curriculum, I have endeavored to reach conclusions which would be useful rather than merely original. In addition to the main task, I have also been interested in attempting to define the more general term "biblical theology," which currently is in danger of becoming a partisan catchword rather than the name of a scientific discipline.

I wish to take this opportunity to express my gratitude to Professor Fleming James, under whom I began my study of the Old Testament; to Professor Millar Burrows, whose wise and generous counsel guided me in preparing the much more extensive doctoral dissertation which underlies this work; and to my wife, who typed the manuscript.

ROBERT C. DENTAN

Berkeley Divinity School
April 10, 1949

CONTENTS

CONTENTS

PART I

THE HISTORY
OF OLD TESTAMENT THEOLOGY
AS A THEOLOGICAL DISCIPLINE

I

THE BACKGROUND AND ORIGIN
OF THE DISCIPLINE

"Old Testament theology" is one part of a greater discipline called "biblical theology" and cannot be studied in isolation from the larger subject. This is particularly true when dealing with origins, since it was not possible to conceive of Old Testament theology as a separate branch of biblical studies until the idea of biblical theology had been clearly formulated. Thus it becomes necessary to examine first of all the various ways in which the term biblical theology has been used and the manner in which it finally came to mean what it did throughout the nineteenth century.

Biblical Theology as the Equivalent
of "Biblical Studies"

In itself, the term biblical theology might be used to designate a variety of subjects and has in fact been used historically in several different senses. It can, for example, be used to describe the whole field of biblical or exegetical studies as distinguished from other branches of the theological curriculum.[1] The term itself first appears in Calovius' *Systematic Theology* (1655) and is there used in this quite general sense.[2]

1. As in L. Noack, *Die biblische Theologie* (1853) and in T. Heck, *The Curriculum of the Major Seminary* (Washington, 1935).
2. See D. G. C. von Cölln, *Biblische Theologie*, I, 18.

Biblical Theology as a System of Doctrine Based on Biblical Principles

A second and more significant use of the term is to designate a theological system which professes to be drawn from the Bible alone, without admixture of concepts drawn from pure reason or speculative philosophy. Such a theology would stand in contrast to the theology of the historic creeds and confessions in regarding the Bible alone as the norm of faith. Although this use of the term is comparatively rare in the eighteenth and nineteenth centuries, it is often so used at the present time, when there is increasing insistence that Christian theology must be based upon biblical revelation rather than upon the insights of Greek philosophy, and expressed in biblical categories rather than in categories drawn from Platonic or Aristotelian metaphysics. Since it was the avowed purpose of the sixteenth-century reformers to return to the pure religion of the Bible, it may seem strange that they did not coin the phrase and use it in this sense. They did not, however, and many elements in their theological thought were, indeed, not derived from the Bible directly, but were simply a part of the common philosophical heritage of the Christian church.

The first serious attempt to escape entirely from the influence of tradition and historic confessions of faith and to theologize in a purely biblical manner was that of Cocceius (1603-69), the inaugurator of the theological school known as the "Federal theology," which persisted in continental religious circles for a century or more.[3] Its main principle was the exposition of God's dealings with men solely in terms of the various "covenants" (*foedera*) which are recorded in Scripture. This school did not actually use the term "Biblical theol-

---

3. Ludwig Diestel, *Geschichte des Alten Testamentes in der christlichen Kirche* (Jena, 1869), pp. 527-530.

ogy" to describe its system of thought, but the Federal theology is nevertheless one of the important historical antecedents of contemporary theological biblicism. Today such a doctrinal system would undoubtedly be termed biblical theology.

A movement similar to the Federal theology in its biblical emphasis was the Pietism of Spener (1635-1705),[4] which represented a strong reaction against the arid scholasticism of the confessional systems and advocated a return to the vital religion which was believed to flow directly from the Bible. The Pietists, however, were temperamentally disinclined toward intellectual speculation and were chiefly interested in the practical and devotional use of the Bible, so their movement can hardly be said to have led to the rise of a new theology, "biblical" or otherwise, although the general influence of Pietism on biblical theology cannot be disregarded, even at the present day.

Toward the end of the eighteenth century, G. C. Storr attempted to counter the destructive effects of the new philosophical spirit of the age upon orthodox doctrine by developing a system of theology from the Scriptures alone, and thereby became the founder of the theological tendency known as the "Older Tübingen School." He treated ecclesiastical dogma with great freedom, but held very closely to biblical supernaturalism and created his theological system by piecing together detached biblical texts "in the fashion of a mosaic." [5] Even as late as 1840 his influence was unmistakable in the posthumous *Biblische Glaubenslehre* of G. C. Knapp, a work which is clearly stamped with the mark of Pietism also.

---

4. *Ibid.,* p. 709; von Cölln, *op. cit.,* p. 120.
5. Otto Pfleiderer, *The Development of Theology in Germany since Kant,* trans. by J. F. Smith (London, 1890), p. 86.

Biblical Theology as a Means of Supporting Orthodox Doctrine

These three efforts at creating a theology based upon purely biblical principles are of interest and importance for an understanding of similar movements in contemporary theology, but actually have no great significance for the rise of the theological discipline which came to be called biblical theology. This arose rather within the framework of the university and theological school, out of the practical need of providing the student of theology with collections of "proof-texts" designed to set forth, in systematic form, the biblical authority for the doctrines of the evangelical church. Naturally, such texts would be accompanied by appropriate exegesis and comment. Since these works were ancillary to the teaching of systematic theology, the arrangement of the materials was dependent upon the traditional order in which the various subjects of that discipline were arranged. This fact is not without importance since biblical theologies to the present day often follow this conventional order. In such works there was no attempt to distinguish sharply the religious ideas of the Old and New Testaments, much less to discriminate times and authors. The Bible was treated as though written by a single author. The principal books of this type were those of Schmid (1671), Hülsemann (1679), König (1651), Baier (1719), Weissmann (1739), and Zickler (1754).[6] Artificial as was their view of the Bible and wooden as was their treatment of it, such books as these contained the seed of interest from which the study of biblical theology was to develop, and the last of them, a treatise by Carl Haymann (1768), was actually entitled *Biblische Theologie*. This is the first instance in which the term was used in a sense which approximates the modern.

6. See Bibliography.

Biblical Theology as Providing a Basis
for Criticizing Orthodox Doctrine

With this general background in mind, it is now possible to turn directly to the story of how biblical theology emancipated itself from its subordinate status as a mere pedagogical auxiliary of systematic or dogmatic theology and became an independent discipline. This process is inseparably associated with the rise of rationalism. The rational, critical, and skeptical temper of the eighteenth century was bound to affect the study of the Bible. This was first evident in the writings of the English deists, Hobbes, Collins, Whiston, Morgan, and Warburton, all of whom dealt with the Bible as they would with any other collection of human documents. At first their work was regarded with great disfavor in Germany, but from the middle of the century on, the position was rapidly changed and German scholarship took the lead in the new critical study of the Scriptures, especially since English deism failed to create a permanent school of biblical studies and soon collapsed into pure skepticism.

No biblical theology in the modern sense of the term was possible until scholarship generally had abandoned the old hermeneutic principles of *analogia scripturae* and *analogia fidei,* which assumed both the uniformity of religious ideas in the Scriptures and their identity with the doctrines of the orthodox churches. This revolution in hermeneutics was largely the work of Semler (d. 1791) and Ernesti (d. 1781), who insisted that the Bible must be interpreted in a purely *historical* and *grammatical* sense. There now began to appear a series of books which made use of the classical proof-texts independently, and used them, and the Scriptures as a whole, not to support orthodox ecclesiastical doctrine, but to criticize it. A. F. Büsching, a theologian of pietistic tendencies, in his inaugural dissertation at Göttingen (1755), gave what Diestel [7] considers the first sketch of a pure biblical theology, and Büsching's *Epitome theologiae e solis literis sacris concinnatae* (1757) was a tentative attempt to carry out such a program. In W. A. Teller's *Topice sacrae scripturae* (1761), the criticism of orthodoxy became a dominant motive and the author made exclusive use of the exegetical principles of Semler and Ernesti, although he retained the old dogmatic framework and treated the Bible as a uniform whole. More radical yet was the *Versuch eines biblischen Systemes der Dogmatik* (1769) of K. F. Bahrdt, a curious eighteenth-century character whose morals seem to have been as loose as his opinions.

A work similar to that of Teller, both in its virtues and its defects, was W. F. Hufnagel's *Handbuch der biblischen Theologie* (1785-89). The author stated that his purpose was to teach his pupils to think for themselves, not to accept blindly either traditional doctrine or the unsupported assertions of their teachers.[8] To this end, he proposed to examine the classical proof-texts with a view to discovering what was the plain meaning intended by the original author.[9] "The proof-texts," he said, "must be used to correct the theological system, not the system the proof-texts." [10] Although Hufnagel was unable to complete his work, the plan of organization which he projected for the whole was an adaptation of the ancient threefold theological pattern of theology, anthropology, and soteriology, a method which was long to remain dominant even in the later development of biblical theology. It is still used, for example, in the recent Old Testament theologies of Koehler and Sellin.

Although Teller and Hufnagel made great progress in the direction of a scientific study of the religious ideas of the Bible,

7. Diestel, *op. cit.*, p. 563.
8. W. F. Hufnagel, *Handbuch der biblischen Theologie,* Preface, pp. xiv-xv.
9. *Ibid.*, pp. xix ff.
10. *Ibid.*, p. xxvi.

as compared with the older collections of proof-texts, they fell considerably short of realizing the true task of biblical theology in that they were still dominated primarily by dogmatic interests (even when they criticized dogma), dealt with their subject in a fragmentary way, and did not clearly distinguish Testaments, books, or sources. However, a book which had appeared ten years before Hufnagel's seems to stand at the point of transition between the old dogmatic interest in the proof-texts and the science of biblical theology which was shortly to be born. This was the *Biblische Theologie* (1775) of G. T. Zachariae. Zachariae wished to popularize the results of scientific study and use them for the clarification of the religious ideas of the "common Christian." [11] He believed that the obligation to study the Bible freely was higher than that of loyalty to the confessional symbols of Lutheranism, although he was also convinced that an honest comparison of biblical ideas would not serve to discredit any of the principal doctrines of the Lutheran church.[12] He deliberately abandoned the method of studying isolated *dicta probantia* in favor of an attempt to study the teaching of the Bible as a whole. In the arrangement of the material for such a project, he insisted that one must follow a plan derived from the nature of the Bible itself, and not one based upon "a method of theological classifications used elsewhere in systems and compendiums." [13] Although Zachariae's book represents a great improvement over the works previously mentioned, it still failed to be a treatise on biblical theology in the later sense, since the author's center of interest was still in the theological system which he hoped to purify rather than in the Bible for its own sake. Moreover, in spite of his announced intention,[14] he still failed to distinguish with any degree of thoroughness different times and different authors.

11. G. T. Zachariae, *Biblische Theologie,* p. 14.   12. *Ibid.,* pp. 16, 24 f.
13. *Ibid.,* Introduction, p. v.   14. *Ibid.,* p. vi.

Biblical Theology
as an Independent Historical Discipline

The latter half of the eighteenth century was the point of crystallization of many previous tendencies. It was the age of Semler's works on exegesis, of the great works of Lowth and Herder on the literary appreciation of the Old Testament and of Eichhorn's epoch-making *Introduction to the Old Testament*. The keynote of all these books, as of many others of smaller stature, was the liberation of biblical studies from the tyranny of dogmatic interests. It was inevitable that this should culminate in a demand for the independent study, not only of literary, historical, and exegetical questions, but of the *religion* of the Bible. The first suggestion of such a demand is to be found in J. G. Hoffmann's *Oratio de theologiae biblicae praestantiae* (1770),[15] but later writers unanimously see the actual beginning of the new discipline of biblical theology in the lecture entitled *"Oratio de iusto discrimine theologiae biblicae et dogmaticae regundisque recte utriusque finibus,"* given by Johann Philipp Gabler to inaugurate his professorship in theology at the University of Altdorf, March 30, 1787. It was Gabler's conviction that the confusion existing in the Christian world was largely due to the improper use of the Bible, which arose in part at least from the failure to discriminate between the complex ideas of dogmatic theology and the simple ideas of biblical religion. He proposed, therefore, to distinguish sharply between biblical theology, which treats of the simple religion of the Bible, and dogmatic theology, which, although based upon materials drawn from biblical theology, also makes use of philosophy and of ideas which arose in the later development of the Christian church.[16] "Biblical theology," he says,

15. von Cölln, *op. cit.*, p. 23.
16. J. P. Gabler, *"Oratio . . . ,"* p. 182.

"is historical in character and sets forth what the sacred writers thought about divine matters; dogmatic theology, on the contrary, is didactic in character, and teaches what a particular theologian philosophically and rationally decides about divine matters, in accordance with his character, time, age, place, sect or school, and other similar influences." [17] Gabler advocated a technique of study involving three stages: first, the biblical theologian must interpret the individual passages of Scripture, using purely grammatical and historical principles. Second, he will compare these with each other, noting carefully points of agreement and disagreement. Third, he will endeavor to formulate such general ideas as he can, without distorting his materials or obliterating distinctions. Upon this firm, scientific foundation of biblical theology, the systematic theologian will then be able to erect a superstructure of dogmatic theology accommodated to the needs of his own time.[18]

It was Gabler who first showed that biblical and dogmatic theology are neither to be confused with each other, nor set in irreconcilable opposition, but are two clearly separable and equally necessary steps in the formulation of a Christian view of the world. This separation of functions was of momentous consequence both for dogmatics and for biblical studies, and every subsequent attempt to obscure the distinction which Gabler made has resulted only in confusion in both fields.

17. *Ibid.,* pp. 183 f.
18. *Ibid.,* pp. 190-193.

II

THE AGE OF RATIONALISM

Gabler was a rationalist, and for nearly fifty years the new theological discipline which he had defined and inaugurated was to be cultivated almost exclusively by men of that school. The first writers in the field—C. F. Ammon, G. L. Bauer, and G. P. C. Kaiser—were the most colorful characters to appear in the whole history of the subject.

C. F. Ammon, whose *Biblische Theologie* appeared (1792) five years after Gabler's famous address and was directly indebted to it, was the greatest rationalist theologian and one of the most brilliant scholars of his age, although he had an offensive habit of changing his theological views to accord with the temper of the times and the changes in political administration. Schleiermacher accused him of shifting about like an eel on a slippery deck.[1] Like many rationalists, he was by no means convinced that the bald results of a purely scientific discipline such as biblical theology ought to be communicated directly to the public, but rather regarded it as an esoteric pursuit for the scholarly, which might prove dangerous to established religion and the accepted order of society if its conclusions became too quickly and too generally known.[2] Although the arrangement of the material in his book was conventional, consisting of the discussion of the more important classical prooftexts, arranged according to the traditional rubrics of dogmatic

1. See Herzog, *Realencyclopädie*, I, 454.
2. C. F. Ammon, *Biblische Theologie*, pp. xiii f., 17-20.

theology, he defined biblical theology as "a science altogether independent of dogmatics." [3] One of its principal functions, he believed, was to combat the "mystical flights into the clouds" of persons who, ignorant of the sources of their religion, were in danger of alienating the best minds of the nation.[4] In dealing with the material, his method was that of an uncompromising rationalism. For Ammon, "the figurative expression 'revelation' is one of the most ambiguous and obscure ideas in theology," and, so far as he is concerned, the only test of revelation is that it agrees with reason. "We must not claim inspiration for these writings before we have tested their rationality and proved it incontrovertibly." [5] The primary duty of the biblical theologian, he says, is "to study the Scriptures for himself, to test everything and to hold fast to that which is good." [6] Since the Bible was written with certain local and temporary circumstances in mind and is the product of the oriental spirit which tends to clothe its ideas in "fantastic" form, it is impossible to construct from it a scientific and harmonious system of Christian belief, but this must not lead the interpreter to take refuge in any dogmatism or in any kind of allegorical or "moral" [7] exegesis. Having arranged the biblical authors in their proper chronological sequence and taken due note of their personal characteristics and those of the age for which they wrote, it is the task of the biblical theologian to give exact "philosophical" information about the results of his study, carefully separating those things which had value as revelation for their age alone from those which are universally valid.[8] The principal divisions of Ammon's book are: God, Creation and Providence, Christ, Soteriology, and Eschatology, each section covering the entire

3. *Ibid.*, pp. xv f.
4. *Ibid.*, pp. xvi f.
5. *Ibid.*, pp. xv f.
6. *Ibid.*, pp. xvi f.
7. Kant was the chief proponent of "moral" exegesis.
8. Ammon, *op. cit.*, pp. 8 f.

Bible, although a separate section on the "Christology of the Old Testament" represents a first tentative step toward an independent treatment of Old Testament theology.

The first work to be completely independent of dogmatic theology, not only with respect to its conclusions but even its *interests,* was G. L. Bauer's *Theologie des Alten Testaments* (1796). Bauer was the first (with the partial exception of Zachariae) to break completely with the method of commenting on proof-texts, and his book may therefore be regarded as the first real treatise on biblical theology in Gabler's sense of the term. Bauer had no concern with the use which systematic theologians might make of his book. His one interest, as the subtitle indicates, was to give a sketch of "the religious ideas of the ancient Hebrews." One notes immediately the radical separation he makes between the Old and New Testaments[9] and, within his book, the careful separation of documents, periods, and persons. As immediate ends which can be served by Old Testament theology he mentions the following: First, the student will be preserved from the error of attributing to the ancient Hebrews ideas which are only doctrines of Christian theology. Second, Old Testament theology will prepare him for the study of the biblical theology of the New Testament, since the Old Testament is the ground upon which the New Testament is built. Finally, it will have apologetic value, inasmuch as it will show the great superiority of the Christian religion to that of the Old Testament. The period to be covered by Old Testament theology he conceived to be that which extends from the earliest beginnings of the Hebrew religion down to the establishment of Christianity, and the sources to be used include the Apocrypha and the writings of Judaism as well as the Old Testament. The method should be that of fearless search for truth regardless of consequences. Much chaff will have to be thrown away, but that which is of positive

9. Four years later he turned to the study of New Testament theology.

value can only be benefited by the process. His principle of organization was based upon the common-sense answer to the question, "What is it we wish to know about the religion of any individual or nation?" Do we not wish to know how it conceives of God and his relation to man, and how it conceives of man and his relation to God? Thus the two major divisions of the subject are: (I) Theology, and (II) Anthropology. Unfortunately, Bauer, like all other writers on the subject, found that some of the material resists any such simple classification and he was forced to add two long appendices on Angels and Demons. His point of view in the interpretation of the material was naïvely rationalistic. Any idea of supernatural revelations of God through theophanies, miracles, or prophecies is to be rejected, since such things are contrary to sound reason and can easily be paralleled amongst other peoples. Thus Bauer regarded Moses as a brave, intelligent man, well instructed in the wisdom of Egypt, whose high purposes were strengthened when he saw a bush which had been kindled by lightning in a thunderstorm.[10] In common with the entire rationalist school and in spite of their expressed desire to read the Bible in the light of its time, Bauer's whole tendency was to interpret the religion of Israel in terms of quasi-philosophical concepts rather than to appreciate the unique quality of the Hebrew mind. Much that is most characteristic and valuable in the Old Testament he regarded simply as a product of the "fantastic" oriental mind. The chief criticism of the work made by Bauer's contemporaries was that he failed to write a *history* of Israel's religion. Feeling the force of this, he published in 1801 his *Beilagen zur Theologie des Alten Testaments,* an even more rationalistic work than the original treatise. His history was very superficial inasmuch as he simply divided the Old Testament into fourteen sections, separating Genesis from the rest of the Pentateuch, Joshua from Judges, etc., and dealt

10. G. L. Bauer, *Theologie des Alten Testaments,* p. 114.

with the religious ideas of each. Nevertheless, this was the first
effort to write a history of the religion of Israel, and thus we
see at the very beginning of our subject the emergence of those
two methods of treating Old Testament religion—the synoptic
and the genetic—which, in our own day, have actually become
two separate disciplines. In addition to the works mentioned,
Bauer also wrote a *Hebräische Mythologie des Alten und
Neuen Testaments* (1802) and a *Biblischen Moral des Alten
Testaments* (1803).

Easily the most curious work in the whole history of the subject is *Die biblische Theologie* of G. P. C. Kaiser, the first
volume of which appeared in 1813. It marks the *ne plus ultra*
of rationalism as well as the first systematic attempt to apply
the *religionsgeschichtlich* method to the interpretation of the
Bible. With all their rationalism, previous writers had at least
paid lip service to the doctrine of the finality of the Christian
religion. With Kaiser the last such pretense disappears. For
him, the idea of particular revelation seemed irrational and
impious. The Bible was chiefly of interest as giving concrete
instances of the application of universal laws. This principle
determined Kaiser's general course of procedure, which was:
first, to develop a general law or to show the universality of
certain phenomena, and then, second, to illustrate this from the
Bible. For example, the lowest stage of human religion is that
of fetichism (which he calls *"Geofetissologie"*!), the worship
of inanimate natural objects. This stage is illustrated in the
Bible by the *teraphim,* Jacob's stone, the fiery pillar of Moses,
and the personified natural forces which later Judaism and
Christianity call by the name of angels.[11] He hoped through
his work to separate those ideas in the Bible which are universally true from those which are merely *Zeitideen,* and so to
lay the foundations for the universal religion of the future—
a religion whose temples would be consecrated to such things

11. G. P. C. Kaiser, *Die biblische Theologie,* I, 59 f.

as Mother Love, Married Bliss, Friendship, etc.; whose feasts would celebrate the annual round of nature as well as the birthdays of the founders of great religions; and whose canon of Scripture would be large enough to include all the great spiritual writings of the past, present, and future.[12] He divided his work into three volumes: the first dealing with the idea of God, Creation, Providence, and Man; the second dealing with the Cultus; and the third, with Morality. One of the most curious things about this curious work is that Kaiser's religious convictions underwent a complete transformation between volumes two and three. In the preface to the third volume, which is written entirely from a conservative theological point of view, he declares that "the Word revealed in the Bible has become for me something entirely unique."[13] One cannot but wonder whether his appointment, during the same interval, to the chair of theology at Erlangen, may not have had something to do with his sudden conversion!

A definite movement away from the spirit of "vulgar rationalism" which had hitherto dominated the field of biblical theology became apparent in the *Biblische Dogmatik* of W. M. L. De Wette which was published in the same year as Kaiser's first volume (1813). It was De Wette's purpose, in all his theological writing, to rise above both orthodoxy and rationalism to a higher unity of faith and religious feeling. His general theological position profoundly affected his treatment of biblical theology, which is marked, in contrast to that of his immediate predecessors, both by genuine religious depth and a philosophical spirit. Indeed, with respect to this latter point, it is one of the fundamental defects of this book (as of De Wette's theological work in general) that it is so largely based on the philosophical system of his personal friend, the Kantian thinker, Jacob Fries. Revelation, for De Wette, meant "any true religious idea expressed in language or symbol." Such true ideas

12. *Ibid.*, II, 232-242.   13. *Ibid.*, III, 4.

cannot appear, however, without the Spirit of God working through the reason, which must be always conscious of dependence upon a higher power.[14] For him biblical theology was not a mere historical discipline, even though it must proceed by historical methods. Its task was not merely to picture the historic biblical faith, but to show its universal and rational inner essence, stripped of all local, temporary, and merely symbolic ideas, and furthermore to transmit its typical religious "feeling" (*Gefühl*), since the characteristic life of religion "consists in feeling, and the forms under which it expresses itself in purest fashion are esthetic forms." [15] This important subject of the mood of Old Testament piety was hardly to be touched upon again until, in our day, Hempel dealt with it exhaustively in his *Gott und Mensch im Alten Testament*. In the arrangement of the material, De Wette believed the principle to be followed must be derived from the character of the religion and not based upon a preconceived logical scheme, or consist merely of a series of loosely ordered rubrics. "Every religion will have a basic idea, from which all else depends, and must be ordered in accordance with it." [16] He found the basic principle of Hebraism (the ancient Hebrew religion as opposed to Judaism, its degenerate offspring) to be "the moral, non-mythical idea of God as a holy will." [17] In conformity with his general principles, he divided his treatment of Old Testament theology under two heads: "Ideal Universalism," which deals with the fundamental doctrines of God, Angels, and Men, and "Symbolic Particularism," which treats of the idea and institutions of the theocracy. It was the distinctive contribution of De Wette that he was the first to combine biblical theology with a particular system of philosophy, a method of treatment which was to be carried to the ultimate extreme by the writers who will be the subject of the next chapter, and which is fa-

14. W. M. L. De Wette, *Biblische Dogmatik*, p. 25.
15. *Ibid.*, p. 20.   16. *Ibid.*, pp. 38 f.   17. *Ibid.*, p. 64.

miliar to us in our day from the widespread tendency to interpret the Bible in terms of Kierkegaardian Existentialism.

In 1828 L. F. O. Baumgarten-Crusius, professor of theology at Jena, published his *Grundzüge der biblischen Theologie*. His work represented an even more definite reaction against the barrenness of vulgar rationalism and can be included in a section devoted to rationalism only because the book exhibits no specific theological character of its own. An orthodox countermovement was to come, but it did not arrive with this book. Baumgarten-Crusius was a mild man who refused to identify himself with any party, although his theology was closely related to that of Schelling and Schleiermacher. His book bears the imprint of his character and may indeed be regarded as the first really honest attempt to produce a work which would be completely objective, in the sense of being independent not only of church doctrine, but also of rationalistic prejudices and philosophical presuppositions. He defined the task of biblical theology as that of describing "the ideas and teachings of the writers of the Old and New Testaments about God and human destiny, showing the relationship of the writers to each other in their connection and inner development." [18] "It should compile a system of purely biblical ideas which can serve as a foundation and norm for faith (*Glaubenslehre*), and a point of departure for the history of dogma." [19] He rejected De Wette's name for the discipline, "biblical dogmatics," since that seems to restrict its subject matter to things which can be reduced to speculative form. As a basic unifying principle for the whole religion of the Bible, he proposed the idea of "the Kingdom of God." [20] In the Old Testament, this term refers to the nation of Israel, but in the New Testament to that condition "in which man gives himself utterly to God and expects all from Him." [21] Unfortunately, Baumgarten-Crusius took

18. L. F. O. Baumgarten-Crusius, *Grundzüge der biblischen Theologie*, p. 1.   19. *Ibid.*, p. vii.   20. *Ibid.*, pp. 13, 147 f.   21. *Ibid.*, p. 150.

what many would consider a retrograde step in that he did not deal separately with the Old and New Testaments, perhaps because of his interest in demonstrating the higher unity of Scripture. However, under his separate rubrics, he clearly distinguished Old and New Testament views and had a soundly historical view of their relationship.

In the following year, there appeared the first volume of a monumental work by C. P. W. Gramberg entitled *Kritische Geschichte der Religionsideen des Alten Testaments*. This work does not purport to be a theology of the Old Testament, but is important as standing in the direct line which leads from Bauer's *Beilagen* to the histories of the religion of Israel of the post-Wellhausen era. The particular interest which led Gramberg to write this book was not that of biblical theology, but a desire to prove the correctness of his own theories as to the late date of the work of the Chronicler. His treatment of Israel's religious development was as mechanical and wooden as Bauer's had been, but both in its attempt at complete objectivity and in the brilliance and accuracy of many of its critical judgments, the work was a remarkable anticipation of the point of view which was to prevail at the close of the nineteenth century.

The last work which can, in any sense, be said to belong to the age of rationalism is the *Biblische Theologie* of D. C. von Cölln (1836), which was long to remain the most popular work on the subject. Though in many respects von Cölln was strongly influenced by De Wette, he rejected the latter's name for the discipline ("biblical dogmatics"), since the Bible contains no dogmas in the usual sense of "precise definitions of religious ideas under public sanctions" and also because so to define the subject would be to exclude the discussion of morality, which is an inseparable ingredient of biblical religion.[22]

22. D. C. von Cölln, *Biblische Theologie*, p. 6.

He also strongly criticized De Wette's introduction of philosophical ideas into biblical theology and insisted upon the
purely historical character of the discipline. The task of biblical theology, he believed, was not to relate those things which
might accord with a particular philosophical system nor to
demonstrate the rationality of the ideas which it describes. Its
sole concern should be their factual certainty (*factische Ge-
wissheit*).[23] He took up a suggestion, previously made by both
De Wette and Baumgarten-Crusius, that biblical theology is
the first chapter in the History of Doctrine, and used this concept to reinforce his conviction that the sole permissible
method of procedure in both disciplines is the historical. "Both
make use of a method of criticism which is not dogmatic, in
the sense of being concerned with inner truth, but is historical
in the sense of being concerned with the factuality of the
data." [24] He believed that biblical theology should deal with
the religious ideas of the Bible genetically,[25] and thus brought
to light once more that inner tension with regard to method
which was later to lead to the division of biblical theology into
two separate disciplines. The arrangement of the material in
his book is an unsatisfactory compromise between the genetic
and the systematic, or "architectonic," method of presenting
biblical ideas. The actual outline of the work is clearly dependent on that of De Wette. Volume I, which deals with the
"Biblical Theology of the Old Testament," is divided into two
main sections: "Hebraism" and "Judaism," each of which in
turn is divided into sections dealing with "Universalism" and
"Particularism" in the religious thought of each period.

With von Cölln an epoch comes to an end, one marked
either by an extreme and "vulgar" rationalism which saw in
the Old Testament merely an illustration of the progress of religious ideas in accordance with the universal laws of reason,

23. *Ibid.*, p. 11.   24. *Ibid.*, p. 7.   25. *Ibid.*, p. 8.

or by a more moderate rationalism which, while attempting to preserve a scientific objectivity of approach, represented a truly honest effort to reconcile historic Christianity with the thought-forms of the modern age. Other tendencies were already at work and the new generation which began with the second quarter of the century would develop biblical theology along quite different lines. These tendencies were already manifest in the philosophical overtones of De Wette's work and in the moderate conservatism of Baumgarten-Crusius.

III

THE INFLUENCE OF THE
PHILOSOPHY OF RELIGION

The two greatest influences on German intellectual life in the
first half of the nineteenth century were the philosopher Hegel
and the theologian Schleiermacher. It was inevitable that some
repercussions of their influence should be felt in the field of
Old Testament theology. Something of the new intellectual
atmosphere generated by Schleiermacher is evident in the
works mentioned in the previous section, particularly in the
interest which De Wette, and to a lesser extent, von Cölln,
show in religious "feeling," but Schleiermacher's influence
could never be extensive because of the essential subjectivism
of his approach to theology and his unfavorable attitude toward the Old Testament. For him it was merely a historical
accident that Christianity had developed on the soil of Judaism. The case was altogether different with Hegel, whose
philosophical system involved the attempt to explain the whole
of human history. For this, the history of Israel, covering approximately two millennia, offered promising material for
study. Hegel had already given an impetus in this direction by
his *Philosophy of Religion* in which he had assigned to the religion of Israel a defined and necessary place in the development of Christianity, the absolute religion. There are, according to Hegel, three stages in the historical evolution of religion:
(1) the religion of Nature, in which God is regarded as a natural substance; (2) the religion of Spiritual Individuality, in
which God is regarded as Subject (specifically, the Jewish re-

ligion as the religion of Sublimity; the Greek as the religion of Beauty; and the Roman as the religion of Utility); (3) the Absolute, or Christian religion.[1] This view of Hebrew religion, together with Hegel's general historical schematism, offered an almost irresistible temptation to enthusiastic Hegelians who were also students of Scripture to attempt an Old Testament theology in Hegelian terms.

The first to do this was Wilhelm Vatke, a young Privat-dozent at Berlin, who in 1835 published his *Biblische Theologie: Part I,* "Die Religion des Alten Testaments." Both because of the insufferable Hegelian terminology of the first part of the book and because Vatke's critical views were far in advance of his time, the book remained almost unnoticed for over thirty years until its view of the history of Israel was popularized by Wellhausen, who acknowledged that it was from Vatke that he had learned "the most and the best." [2] According to Vatke, "Biblical theology presents the idea of religion in the form in which it constituted the basic consciousness of the Hebrew people and the primitive age of Christianity. In other words, it presents the religious and ethical conceptions of the Holy Scriptures in their historical development and inner connection." [3] Again, in more Hegelian language, he says that its purpose is to set forth "the living movement of biblical religion, its general concept (*Begriff*), its subjective and historical manifestation, and its Idea." [4] He regarded the previous "rationalistic" period in the development of biblical theology as necessary, but one which had now been superseded. The ideal of perfect scientific objectivity which it had professed he considered neither possible nor desirable. The scholar cannot

1. Friedrich Ueberweg, *History of Philosophy,* Eng. trans. by G. S. Morris (New York, 1872), p. 243; O. Pfleiderer, *The Development of Theology in Germany since Kant,* pp. 76 f.; Diestel, *Geschichte des Alten Testamentes in der christlichen Kirche,* pp. 689 f.
2. Quoted by E. König, *Theologie des Alten Testaments,* p. 4, note.
3. W. Vatke, *Biblische Theologie,* p. 2.   4. *Ibid.,* p. 147.

and should not eliminate the subjective element from his studies, but should consciously choose a standpoint "which regards all the forms of the spiritual life as members of a great organism and seeks to understand every particular standpoint as an integrating moment of the whole." [5] Vatke rejected the idea that biblical theology is distinguished from dogmatics by its concern with mere historical factuality as opposed to the truth of the ideas contained in it. Biblical theology judges of the truth of the ideas it sets forth and "is directly polemic and apologetic." [6] The idea of objective revelation was fundamental to Vatke's thought. The whole historical process in which the Idea of Religion develops is based upon the nature of God, and it is just as much a necessity for God to reveal himself to man, as for man to raise himself out of his own finitude to the highest self-consciousness, which is the standpoint of the Spirit. [7] In the actual arrangement of his work, Vatke adopted a purely historical framework and thus became the third in the line which leads from Bauer's *Beilagen* through Gramberg to the post-Wellhausen school. Although his Hegelian presuppositions led him to adopt a chronological method of presentation, Vatke defended the principle of presenting the material systematically, and rejected the idea that biblical theology can be set forth only in categories derived from the Bible itself, since the books of the Bible are popular in character and *any* system of arrangement must actually be imposed from outside. [8] The first and last sections of his book are written in an opaque Hegelian style, but the middle section, which gives his revolutionary account of the history of Israel's religion, is clearly and simply written and the account itself is essentially the developmental one later championed by Reuss, Graf, and Wellhausen. Vatke's theory, ostensibly based upon the principles of the Hegelian philosophy, was actually founded to a large extent upon sober and penetrating criticism and his own

5. *Ibid.*, p. 14.   6. *Ibid.*, p. 153.   7. *Ibid.*, p. 20.   8. *Ibid.*, pp. 4 f.

remarkable historical intuitions. It was most unfortunate that the book's Hegelian garb condemned it to neglect for considerably more than a theological generation.

So radical a transformation of the traditional idea of the course of Old Testament religion could only arouse the bitterest opposition among scholars, although some features of Vatke's theory had previously been adumbrated in the work of De Wette and Gramberg. For the most part, the book was treated with silent contempt. However, three years after its publication, another huge treatise appeared which attempted to hoist Vatke with his own petard, by using his Hegelian approach to arrive at an opposite conclusion. This was *Die Religion des Alten Testaments in der geschichtlichen Entwickelung ihrer Principien* (1838) of Bruno Bauer, another young Privatdozent at Berlin, who had studied under Vatke. He was one of the most eccentric thinkers in the world of German scholarship and shortly after this underwent that strange transformation of theological character which made his name a byword for extreme and reckless radicalism. In this book, though, his eccentricity manifested itself in an extreme conservatism, supported by a pervasive and all-controlling Hegelianism in viewpoint and vocabulary which is far more deserving the adjective "insufferable" than that of Vatke. No ecclesiastical allegorizing was ever more fantastic than that which appears on page after page of this book, in which all the vividness of actual human history is transformed into the dialectical thrusts and counterthrusts of intellectual phantoms. Bauer's philosophical approach and his arbitrary and fantastic interpretation of the data made it possible for him to demonstrate that every event in the traditional account of Hebrew religious history was the necessary result of "the growing and unfolding self-consciousness of the Absolute Spirit." Bauer's one contribution to Old Testament theology was to demonstrate the futility of attempting to write a history or an interpretation of Hebrew religion in terms derived from Hegel or any other philosophical system. Vatke's book would live because the philosophy was only an unfortunate framework for a view of the history which was essentially sound. Bauer's book suddenly reduced the philosophical approach to the absurd. One's risibilities cannot fail to be stirred by the spectacle of these two doctrinaire Hegelians trudging their way through hundreds of pages of mountainous dialectic from identical presuppositions to diametrically opposite conclusions. While the thought of Hegel would continue in more subtle ways to influence the study of biblical religious history, no one would ever try to write this kind of book again. Faint echoes of explicit Hegelianism are still to be discerned in L. Noack's *Die biblische Theologie* (1853), a general handbook of information about the Bible intended primarily for lay people, but the book itself is of such slight importance in the history of the subject that it can hardly be regarded as an exception.

Although the dominance of Hegel's philosophy of religion and history in Old Testament theology was of such short duration, this brief interlude had a positive contribution to make in that it raised the level of discussion above the mere description of observable facts to an attempt to see the nature of the deep, underlying causes. The Hegelians thus contributed a certain philosophical mood to biblical theology without which its interests are likely to appear merely trivial and antiquarian. Also, they rightly insisted that Hebrew religion cannot be understood apart from the concept of historical development, and that that development is not simply a matter of chronological successiveness, but of organic growth.

IV

THE CONSERVATIVE REACTION

During the first four decades after Gabler had defined the task of biblical theology, orthodox theological scholarship stood aloof from the discipline. Considering the fact that even before Gabler's time, books on "biblical theology" had been written as a means of criticizing the doctrines of the churches,[1] this is scarcely to be wondered at. Further, Gabler's program ran counter to a basic assumption of Protestant orthodoxy, viz., that the theology of the Bible and that of the ecclesiastical confessions were identical. Following a familiar pattern, however, the conservative theological world which had originally opposed the new technique, eventually tolerated it and finally adapted it to its own ends. Conservative biblical scholarship at last came to see that biblical theology is not necessarily incompatible with a devout acceptance of the Scriptures as inspired or even inerrant. Baumgarten-Crusius had pointed out that, theoretically, such a discipline might have arisen in any age of the Christian church.[2] We have already noted a distinct reaction toward more conservative views among the last representatives of the age of rationalism, and there could be little doubt that a time was rapidly approaching when a thoroughly conservative biblical theology could be written. This time coincided roughly with the beginning of that great reactionary

1. See *supra,* pp. 19 f.
2. L. F. O. Baumgarten-Crusius, *Grundzüge der biblischen Theologie,* p. 3.

movement in politics as well as theology which characterized the middle decades of the nineteenth century. With the important exception of the works mentioned in the last section, the next period in the history of Old Testament theology was dominated by men of conservative and even reactionary views.

A first tentative effort in this direction is to be seen in a work which is a landmark of orthodox Old Testament scholarship, E. W. Hengstenberg's *Christologie des Alten Testaments* (1829-35). Although this work is not an Old Testament theology, since it deals merely with the Messianic prophecies, it is epoch-making in that its publication marks a vigorous reawakening of the strictly orthodox view of the Old Testament Scriptures, one which rejects any real idea of progress in revelation, hardly distinguishes between the Testaments, and gives a "spiritual" interpretation to the Old Testament prophecies which almost ignores any consideration of their original reference.

The first complete work on Old Testament theology produced by the conservative school was, however, a work which exhibited a more flexible variety of orthodoxy than that of Hengstenberg. This was a volume of *Vorlesungen über die Theologie des Alten Testaments* by J. C. F. Steudel, posthumously edited by his pupil, G. F. Oehler (1840). Steudel was accustomed in his academic lectures to deal with the material first genetically and then systematically, and was apparently the first to divide the subject matter in this way. Only the lectures belonging to the second half of his course are included in the published work. Oehler classifies him theologically as a "rational supernaturalist." [3] Certainly Steudel regarded the Old Testament as of divine origin, although he specifically rejected the doctrine of "verbal" inspiration.[4] His critical views would be regarded today as extremely conservative. Nevertheless, for

3. In a biographical article in Herzog, *Realencyclopädie*.
4. J. C. F. Steudel, *Vorlesungen über die Theologie des Alten Testaments*, pp. 44-51, 64.

him, as for the rationalists, Old Testament theology was an objective science and the only legitimate method of exegesis was the grammatical-historical. "It is not our concern," he says, "to present the content of the Old Testament dogmatically, i.e., for the purpose of giving definite form to our own convictions, but historically, in order to understand the religious conceptions which were extant at a particular period." [5] He was strongly critical of the subjectivity of the Hegelians and insisted that a reasonable objectivity—such as we assume when we endeavor sincerely to understand another person's point of view—is easily within the capacity of rational men. [6] Although the part of his lectures which appeared in print covers the religion of the Old Testament systematically, Steudel was inclined to believe that the historical, chronological approach was better, [7] and, of course, his pedagogical method presupposed that the student would already have studied the material from the genetic point of view. This preference for the historical approach was undoubtedly due to his emphasis upon the idea of progressive revelation. [8] In outlining the systematic portion of his lectures, he followed, with slight modifications, the traditional threefold scheme of God, Man, and Salvation.

A more rigidly uncompromising orthodoxy is to be found in the *Vorlesungen über die Theologie des Alten Testaments* (1848) of H. A. C. Hävernick, another posthumous volume. The author was a young professor of great promise at Königsberg who died prematurely at the age of thirty-four. Although a pupil, and to some extent a follower of Hengstenberg, he admitted significant modifications in his master's point of view, particularly by giving larger scope to the idea of development. The rigidity of Hävernick's conservatism appears chiefly in his uncritical treatment of the sources. His theories with regard to Old Testament theology are, on the other hand, remarkably fresh and stimulating. He demands the use of objective his-

5. *Ibid.*, p. 70.   6. *Ibid.*, pp. 79 f.   7. *Ibid.*, pp. 65 f.   8. *Ibid.*, pp. 66 ff.

torical methods in the study of the material, but at the same time insists that these by themselves will not produce adequate results. A merely impartial approach to the Bible will, he says, give a distorted picture of the subject. The student must have a "theological aptitude" which can be won only by religious belief and experience, by "love, self-surrendering love." [9] With regard to the idea of revelation, he declares that God reveals himself in the Old Testament not in abstract ideas but "in a series of acts which form an organic, developing whole." [10] Therefore the *ideas* of Old Testament religion must not be treated in isolation from its *history*. This history has no obvious unity within itself, but finds its unifying principle in the final act, the appearance of God in Christ.[11] At the same time he strongly criticizes the older orthodoxy for having tried to find Christ everywhere in the small details of the Old Testament text rather than seeing him as the culmination of a great historical movement.[12] In view of Hävernick's acceptance of the idea of development, it was natural that he, like Steudel, should feel that only a genetic approach to the religion of the Old Testament could really do justice to its essential character. Actually, though, the main part of the book shows little influence of his theory and follows a systematic scheme of discussion under the three traditional heads.

Hävernick's is not the only book on Old Testament theology in which the theory is better than the practice. His mind, like that of many of his predecessors and successors, was torn between two conceptions of the discipline, the one historical or genetic, the other systematic or architectonic. Only Steudel had as yet perceived that both methods are legitimate and necessary and the historical approach is not a substitute for, but an essential preliminary to, the systematic treatment. Unfortunately, it was not yet possible to write a credible history of the

9. H. A. C. Hävernick, *Vorlesungen über die Theologie des Alten Testaments,* p. 4.   10. *Ibid.,* pp. 14 f., 17.   11. *Ibid.*   12. *Ibid.,* p. 114.

religion of Israel, since the course of its development was as yet unknown, and this fact undoubtedly contributed to the confusion as to the general method by which it should be presented. As long as the fully developed priestly Law was regarded as standing at the beginning of that history, it was impossible to trace any genuine development. Such writers as Hävernick and his greater successor, Oehler, were, partly due to the Hegelian spirit of the age, thoroughly sympathetic to the idea of development, but until Vatke's remarkable intuitions as to the late date of the priestly material had been vindicated by Wellhausen and others, it was possible to introduce that idea into their picture of Israel's history only in a theoretical and artificial way.

There can be no doubt that G. F. Oehler was the greatest name in Old Testament theology in the first three quarters of the nineteenth century. His first work was a slim volume entitled *Prolegomena zur Theologie des Alten Testaments* (1845), the first and only work to deal exclusively with the theory and method of Old Testament theology. Although extremely conservative in his critical views, Oehler was profoundly influenced by Hegel and frankly declares that one can learn more from the philosophers of religion than from many supposedly "theological" discussions of the Old Testament.[13] This led him to criticize his teacher, Steudel, for having conceived of the development of Hebrew religion in terms of quantitative addition rather than of organic growth. Oehler insists that it is a part of the function of Old Testament theology to discover "the Idea" which is the objective basis for the organic life of Old Testament religion. This Idea he would define in terms of the divine Spirit which by gradual, progressive revelation produced the historical movement culminating in the life of Jesus Christ. Since in every living thing it is the apex of development which determines the course of development, he

13. G. F. Oehler, *Prolegomena zur Theologie des Alten Testaments,* p. x.

feels it can be truly said that the Spirit which is the objective principle of the Old Testament is none other than the Spirit of Christ.[14] Like Hävernick, Oehler criticized the older supernaturalism for thinking of revelation as the communication of higher knowledge. "Old Testament religion is rather mediated through a series of divine acts and commands and through the institutions of a divine state." [15] This emphasis, along with his interest in the concept of development, naturally led Oehler to advocate the use of the genetic approach and to a partial adoption of it in his own treatment of the subject. Although Oehler held so strongly to a belief in the revealed character of Old Testament religion, he held equally fast to the conception of Old Testament theology as a historical discipline, the task of which is to describe Old Testament religion as a phenomenon in history, and to grammatical-historical exegesis as the only legitimate method of interpretation.[16] While he insisted on scientific objectivity in the biblical theologian, he also insisted that, to be *truly* objective, one must grasp not only the facts of time and place but also penetrate into the "life-order which stands over the causal-nexus," [17] in other words, must understand "the Idea." Oehler asserts this to be necessary for the understanding of any process in history, as important for the history of art or of Greek philosophy as for the theology of the Old Testament, and it is only in this sense that he would admit of anything like a "theological" method of interpretation. Exegesis can be theological only in the sense that it acknowledges the Spirit of Christ as the objective principle of Old Testament religion, since Christ is the goal of the entire process. Like many another writer, Oehler was better able to formulate a theory of Old Testament theology than to produce a treatise on the subject. His posthumous and massive *Theologie des Alten Testaments* (1873), long the most popular book in the field, is today almost completely outmoded, largely because

14. *Ibid.*, pp. 79 f.   15. *Ibid.*, p. 6.   16. *Ibid.*, p. 78.   17. *Ibid.*, p. 79.

Oehler attempted to deal with the material genetically in an age when the genesis of Israel's religion was not understood. He divided his subject into three parts: Mosaism, Prophetism, and Wisdom. The first two parts contain a historical section followed by a systematic section, while the last part contains only a systematic section. Because he misconceived the course of development, considerably more than half the book is devoted to "Mosaism" and much of this consists of archaeological information which by common consent[18] does not properly belong to the field of Old Testament "theology." One interesting methodological feature is that his last chapter is a discussion of Ecclesiastes, as illustrating the ultimate dilemma of Old Testament religion and the need for the Gospel to resolve it. Much the most valuable part of the book is the preface, which is a slightly revised edition of the *Prolegomena*, written thirty years previously. This is still worth reading. The main body of the work seems far more antiquated today than does Volume I of von Cölln's book, which had long been the most popular treatise on the subject. This impression is due to the fact that von Cölln adhered more strictly to the systematic method in the presentation of his material. This fact in itself contains a moral! One incidental point of interest about Oehler's *Theology of the Old Testament* is that it was the first such work to be translated into English (1874-75 and 1883), a fact which indicates a significant stirring of new life at this period amongst English-speaking biblical scholars.

Two years after the publication of Oehler's *Prolegomena*, the Swiss theologian J. L. S. Lutz published his *Biblische Dogmatik* (1847). His conception of the subject was directly opposite to that of Oehler, in that he believed it his task to present the religion of the Bible "in its system." [19] He deliberately chose the title "dogmatics" because he believed that this task involved getting behind the various forms of expression from different periods and trying to discover the "dogmas" or theo-

18. See *infra*, p. 106.   19. J. L. S. Lutz, *Biblische Dogmatik*, p. 1.

retical religious judgments which go together to form the "system" of biblical religion. Lutz denied that "any actual modification of religious ideas can be demonstrated in the different periods." [20] He insisted upon the use of objective, historical method, accompanied by a spiritual relationship on the student's part to the ideas and truths which are to be studied.[21] It is only in the second section of his book, which in part deals with the history of Revelation, that he treated the Old Testament separately.

Similar to Lutz's work in its attempt to deal with the whole field of biblical doctrine, without separation of the Testaments, is Heinrich Ewald's monumental and pretentious *Die Lehre der Bibel von Gott oder Theologie des Alten und Neuen Bundes* (1871-76). Ewald dominated the world of Old Testament studies in the period under discussion, and, although he made enormous contributions to history and linguistic science, Wellhausen credited him with being the one person who for a full generation prevented German scholarship from seeing the true course of Israel's religious history.[22] This book was evidently intended to be his *magnum opus* and appeared in four massive volumes: (I) The Doctrine of the Word of God; (II) and (III) The Doctrine of God and the Universe; and (IV) The Doctrine of the Life of Man and the Kingdom of God. It is another sign of the refertilization of English biblical scholarship after a sterile period of more than a century and a quarter that, a decade later, the first three volumes were translated into English, Volumes II and III under the title of *Old and New Testament Theology*. Almost alone among writers on biblical theology, Ewald regarded the systematic treatment as conforming to the character of the Bible itself and pointed to the Decalogue, Deuteronomy, and Ezekiel 40-48 as evidence of a biblical tendency toward systematization.[23] Although the

20. *Ibid.*, p. 6.   21. *Ibid.*
22. A. Bertholet, article, "Ewald," in *Religion in Geschichte und Gegenwart* (1st ed.), II, 767.
23. H. Ewald, *Old and New Testament Theology*, p. 11.

English translation of this work has recently been reprinted, it is hard to see what appeal it could have for the modern reader, as it is written in a tedious, rhapsodical style, which soars in the realm of poetic generalities, rarely comes to grips with concrete facts, and, as the translator says, contains more of philosophy and mysticism than theology.[24]

The mid-nineteenth century saw not only the rise of a powerful conservative movement in biblical theology regarded as a branch of the theological curriculum, but also a powerful resurgence of biblicism in general theological thought, as a protest against speculative and philosophical tendencies. This is seen particularly in the works of J. C. K. Hofmann,[25] M. Baumgarten, K. A. Auerleben, and Franz Delitzsch. The remote beginnings of the tendency they represent go back to Cocceius and the "Federal theology" in the seventeenth century and also have points of contact with Pietism, although the movement was actually fathered by J. A. Bengel in the eighteenth century and further developed in the writings of F. C. Oetinger and C. A. Crusius. The main principles of the school, according to Diestel,[26] were: the perfect unity and coherence of the Scriptures even in the smallest details; the need of studying the divine economy in its historical development (*Heilsgeschichte*) rather than seeking for a system of "doctrines"; and an emphasis upon the symbolical, typical, and prophetical in the Old Testament Scriptures. The thought of this school (which Diestel, following Hupfeld, calls "biblical theosophy")[27] had considerable influence upon the development of biblical theology strictly so called, and it has obvious parallels in the various "biblical theologies" of the present day.[28]

24. *Ibid.*, p. vi.
25. Hofmann, *Weissagung und Erfüllung* (1841), *Der Schriftbeweis* (1852), *Biblische Hermeneutik* (1880).
26. Diestel, *Geschichte des Alten Testamentes in der christlichen Kirche*, pp. 698-707.   27. *Ibid.*, p. 704, note.
28. Both O. Procksch and G. von Rad, in the mid-20th century, acknowledge their debt to Hofmann. See *infra*, pp. 87 and 93.

Although the general tendencies of the period under consideration were conservative and even reactionary, there were, of course, many individuals lecturing on biblical theology who continued to represent a purely scientific and even rationalizing point of view. Most notable was Eduard Reuss of Strassburg who, as early as 1834, had arrived independently at a position similar to Vatke's, although he published nothing on the subject until 1881. For many, the thirty years which elapsed between the publication of Vatke's ill-fated work and the revival of his theories by Graf seemed a period of black reaction, with the sun of scholarship in eclipse. Regarded otherwise, it was a period of germination, and the way was undoubtedly being prepared for the sudden and startling triumph of Vatke's views. In the meantime, orthodox scholarship was making invaluable contributions to the theory, if not the practice, of Old Testament theology by bringing it into more conscious relationship with Christian thought and feeling, thereby giving it a contemporary, rather than archaeological, relevance, and by giving theological respectability to the Hegelian concept of "organic development."

During this entire period only one work on Old Testament theology was produced by the "rationalistic" school, F. Hitzig's *Vorlesungen über biblische Theologie und messianische Weissagungen des Alten Testaments*. This work, published posthumously in 1880, represents approximately the final form of the lectures on the subject which Hitzig had given on repeated occasions at Zürich and Heidelberg from 1835 to 1874. Hitzig desired to occupy a mediating position between the "negative" school of De Wette on one side and the forces of reaction on the other.[29] So far as this book is concerned, he succeeded only in antagonizing both. Later writers on the subject have nothing good to say of it and it is indeed a curious farrago of rationalism, Pietism, and philosophical speculation.

29. F. Hitzig, *Vorlesungen über biblische Theologie und messianische Weissagungen des Alten Testaments,* p. 15.

V

THE TRIUMPH OF *RELIGIONSGESCHICHTE*

The year 1878, in which Julius Wellhausen published his *Prolegomena zur Geschichte Israels,* marks the beginning of the period which saw the apparent death of Old Testament theology and the rise of a new discipline called "The History of the Religion of Israel." The distinguishing features of the new discipline were its exclusive use of the genetic method and its tendency to treat the religious developments in the Old Testament period as merely particular examples of general *religionsgeschichtlich* laws. We have already observed that from the time of Gabler there had been a tendency in this direction. G. L. Bauer (in the *Beilagen*), Gramberg, Vatke, and Bruno Bauer are striking examples of writers who attempted to produce a history of Israel's religion. It was impossible, however, for this approach to be generally accepted as long as the old, unhistorical view of Israel's religious development prevailed. The true conception had long been advocated by Vatke, and later, Reuss, and in 1866 there began to appear a series of books by such men as Graf, Kuenen, and Duhm, which accepted Vatke's theory of the late origin of the priestly writings. It remained for the lucid, persuasive, and gently humorous pen of Wellhausen to popularize this view. The death of Ewald in 1875 marked the end of an era; the publication of Wellhausen's *Prolegomena* in 1878 marked the beginning of a new one. It was now possible for the first time to write a history of Israel's religion which not only appeared to be justified by a proper understanding of the sources, but also accorded with the intellectual temper of an age which had been taught by Hegel and Darwin to regard the principle of evolution as the magic key to unlock all the secrets of history.

Although the old name is still used in the title, August Kayser's posthumous *Die Theologie des Alten Testaments,* edited and published by Reuss in 1886, marks the point at which the discipline called Old Testament theology gave birth to a new and distinct, though closely related discipline, the "History of the Religion of Israel." Kayser recognized that there were certain advantages in the systematic presentation of the theology of the Old Testament, but felt these advantages were outweighed by the inability of that method to give due importance to the fact of development. Therefore he chose the purely genetic method and frankly says that his work might be more accurately described as "a history of Israelite religion." [1] Some later works still continued to use the name Old Testament theology,[2] but its inappropriateness soon became evident, and, beginning with Smend's *Lehrbuch der alttestamentlichen Religionsgeschichte* (1893), some variation of the latter name was generally adopted for works which dealt with Old Testament religion in a comparative and developmental (*religionsgeschichtlich*) manner. The later productions of this school lie beyond the scope of the present discussion.

Although a new discipline had been born, the old was not yet dead, and the last two decades of the nineteenth century continued to see the production of works which, at least in part, dealt with Old Testament religion systematically. Such works also inclined to take a more definitely religious and theological interest in their subject. Thus in 1889 there appeared

1. A. Kayser, *Die Theologie des Alten Testaments,* p. 3.
2. For example: B. Stade, *Biblische Theologie des Alten Testaments* (1905) and E. Kautzsch's treatment of the religion of Israel in Hastings' *Dictionary of the Bible,* republished in Germany (1911) under the traditional name.

posthumously K. Schlottmann's *Kompendium der biblischen Theologie des Alten und Neuen Testaments*. A large part of the Old Testament section was taken up with purely historical material, but it also contained a systematic account of the "Theocratic Community Consciousness," discussed under the three traditional rubrics: God, Man, and Salvation. Schlottman's view of the history of Israel's religion is startlingly conservative and the book is not an important contribution to the subject. Although E. Riehm's posthumous *Alttestamentliche Theologie* (1889) is of little value as a treatise on the subject, it is important as containing the first attempt to justify the value of Old Testament theology as something distinct from the History of the Religion of Israel. It is, indeed, this attempt to do something different which gives the book its irritating vagueness, since Riehm did not conceive the difference between the two disciplines to lie in the use of the systematic as opposed to the chronological method, but rather to lie in the fact that the History of the Religion of Israel is concerned with mere phenomenology, whereas Old Testament theology is chiefly concerned with the *inner meaning* of the facts and their relationship to the developing organism of the religion of revelation.[3] As one would expect, Riehm insists that "personal religious experience is essential in order to grasp the spirit" of Old Testament religion.[4] He is almost unique among writers on the subject in emphasizing the importance of Old Testament theology in promoting the spiritual life of the Church and in "building the Kingdom of God on earth." [5] Good as his theory is in part, the work as a whole is a failure, because the author failed to see the importance of the systematic, or architectonic, approach to Old Testament religion, and consequently, as Stade[6] says, "moves about the subject in broad and hopeless spirals."

3. E. Riehm, *Alttestamentliche Theologie,* p. 2.
4. *Ibid.,* p. 10.
5. *Ibid.,* pp. vi and 6.
6. Stade, *Biblische Theologie des Alten Testaments,* p. 22.

A more impressive work in every way was the posthumous *Handbuch der alttestamentlichen Theologie* of A. Dillmann, edited and published by R. Kittel in 1895. Though no obscurantist, Dillmann rejected the Wellhausen theory, partly because he felt that the general principle of development was inadequate to account for Israel's religion, since her neighbors, exposed to the same environmental influences, show evidence of no such process. Therefore Israel must have possessed some higher principle from the very beginning.[7] He acknowledged that a purely objective religionsgeschichtlich approach to Hebrew religion was possible, but believed that even this would only disclose the essential uniqueness of the Old Testament in the ancient world and also show that its incompleteness pointed beyond itself to a fulfillment in the Christian Gospel. The Christian, however, he asserted, does not approach the Old Testament with mere objectivity, but regards it as part of his own religion, "flesh of our flesh." [8] It is in this spirit that an Old Testament theology must be written. Amongst the various functions which biblical theology in general can perform, Dillmann speaks of the normative yardstick which it provides for evaluating later theological developments[9] and the notable contribution it should make to the cause of Christian unity.[10] He dealt with his material under three heads: the first, a general section which discusses the uniqueness of the religion of the Old Testament as the religion of "holiness"; the second section, a broad historical outline of Israel's religious development; and the third, a systematic discussion of the religious concepts of Old Testament religion under the three familiar heads.

It might be supposed from the previous discussion that the characteristic methods of Old Testament theology were incompatible with the Wellhausen theory. The two works which remain to be considered in this section show that this is not the case. Both of them accept the new reconstruction of Old Testa-

---

7. A. Dillmann, *Handbuch* . . . , pp. 57-59.
8. *Ibid.,* pp. 8 f.   9. *Ibid.,* p. 3.   10. *Ibid.,* pp. 5 f.

ment religious history and yet endeavor to give a synoptic view of Israel's religious outlook.

This first is C. Piepenbring's *Théologie de l'Ancien Testament* (1886), a work written with typical French lucidity by a pupil of Reuss. Piepenbring attempted a partial accommodation of the systematic to the historical approach, by dividing his book into three historical sections—the Mosaic period, the prophetic period, and the period of Judaism—and then discussing the principal topics of Old Testament religion under each of these heads. The book is of no great originality or depth, and the compromise is not a satisfactory one, but it is important as demonstrating the continued existence, even among orthodox Wellhausians, of a feeling that the permanent elements and basic concerns of Old Testament religion were at least as important as the fact of development.

The greatest work on Old Testament theology in the nineteenth century and almost the only one which can still be read with profit, in spite of its being antiquated in many particulars, is the *Alttestamentliche Theologie* of H. Schultz (five editions, 1869-96). Unlike the many unfortunately posthumous works in the field, the first edition of this book was published while the author was still a young man and antedated Wellhausen's *Prolegomena,* while the last edition, revised by the author, appeared a year later than Dillmann's work. Thus, in its final form, the book is the result of a lifetime of study and experimentation. The various editions are not merely new printings but in some cases represent a radical transformation of the character of the work. This is particularly true of the second (1878) edition, in which Schultz adopted the Wellhausen theory; but even the fifth is a distinct improvement over the fourth,[11] particularly in the direction of greater conciseness. It is clear that Schultz was a scholar of exceptional humility and

11. The fourth edition was translated into English by J. A. Paterson in 1892.

genuine objectivity even toward his own work, and the favorable reception accorded it was no doubt in large degree due to these qualities. However, in addition to these attributes of character, Schultz also had a clear and sound view of the task and method of Old Testament theology. He had no doubt of the revealed character of Old Testament religion, as the subtitle of the book indicates—"The Religion of Revelation in its Pre-Christian Stage of Development." Furthermore, although he was convinced that "biblical theology can be a profitable study only to one who is able to bring himself into a living sympathy with the spirit of that religion," [12] this did not lead him to suppose that theology has some special "method" which distinguishes it from other sciences or that religious faith constitutes a special organ of knowledge. The rules which govern all conscientious historical study must serve here as in other fields.[13] As to the function of biblical theology, he sees it first as offering to systematic theology the materials with which the latter works, providing it with what Schleiermacher demanded, "a form of scripture-proof on a larger scale than individual proof-texts can offer," [14] and then as providing the Church with a measuring stick for later developments.[15] Schultz was also happy in his choice of a unifying principle for biblical religion —the Kingdom of God upon earth.[16] That is not to say that his conception of the Kingdom was adequate, but it did assure that his presentation of the unity of the Bible would not be mystical or theosophical in character, but would be based upon the objective fact of the continuity of developing life, under God's direction, of a historical community. Thus he sees the Old and New Testaments in a vital unity. "It is therefore perfectly clear that no one can expound New Testament theology without a thorough knowledge of Old Testament theology. But it is no less true that one who does not thoroughly understand

12. H. Schultz, *Old Testament Theology,* English trans., I, 11.
13. *Ibid.*   14. *Ibid.,* p. 4.   15. *Ibid.*   16. *Ibid.,* p. 56.

New Testament theology cannot have anything but a one-sided view of Old Testament theology. He who does not know the destination will fail to understand many a bend in the road. For him who has not seen the fruit, much, both in bud and blossom, will always remain a riddle." [17] In arranging his material for the last two editions, Schultz, like Piepenbring, because of his loyalty to the theory of development, adopted a method more ingenious than satisfactory. First he introduced a general discussion of the character of Old Testament religion, then a purely historical account of its development, and finally, a systematic section in which he attempted to present a cross-cut view of the religion of Israel at a particular historical moment, the beginning of the period of the second temple, when presumably the religion had achieved classic form. This pinpointing of the synopsis is highly artificial, but illustrates how difficult the task of organizing the material of Old Testament theology really is.

Schultz's work was the last, as well as the most solid, achievement in the field of Old Testament theology in the nineteenth century. A full quarter of a century would pass before Protestant scholarship in Germany would produce another work similar in plan and purpose.[18] *Religionsgeschichte* had apparently triumphed. It alone corresponded to the scientific temper of the age and the tendency to substitute a philosophy of evolutionary naturalism for revealed religion. Many histories of the religion of Israel would appear, some conservative, some radical, but not even the most conservative would write

17. *Ibid.*, p. 59.
18. In 1908 Father M. Hetzenauer published his *Theologia Biblica,* Vol. I, *Vetus Testamentum,* a significant indication of the revival of biblical studies in the Roman Catholic Church. It treats not only what is ordinarily called biblical theology, but also the secular history of Israel. Although the point of view is necessarily very conservative, it is a work of tremendous learning. The works of P. Scholtz and H. Zschokke listed in the Bibliography are an indication that there was some interest in Old Testament theology among Roman Catholics of the previous century also.

an "Old Testament Theology." Piepenbring and Schultz had demonstrated that Old Testament theology is not essentially incompatible with the new view of Israel's religious origins, but it would require a complete change in the spirit of the age before the old task would really seem worth doing again.

VI

ENGLISH AND AMERICAN WORKS
BEFORE 1920

Little more than an extended footnote is needed to discuss
works on Old Testament theology written in the English language before 1920 since they are few in number and not of
great importance. During the first three quarters of the nineteenth century no works appeared in English dealing with
either Old Testament theology or with biblical theology in general. This was, no doubt, due in large measure to the conservatism of English theological circles and the taint of rationalism
which clung to the development of the idea of biblical theology
in Germany. A marked change set in with the last quarter of
the century. The views of Wellhausen began to find a sympathetic hearing in England,[1] and German books on biblical
theology began to be translated. Thus Oehler's *Old Testament
Theology* was translated in England in 1874-75 and in America in 1883, Ewald's *Die Lehre der Bibel* (abridged) in 1884
and 1888. More radical interests came to the fore with the
publication of a translation of Schultz's *Old Testament Theology* in 1892 and Piepenbring's in the following year.

W. L. Alexander published a work in 1883 in Edinburgh
entitled *A System of Biblical Theology*, but this was actually

1. The publication of Robertson Smith's *The Old Testament in the Jewish
Church* in 1881 was a landmark in Britain similar to that of Wellhausen's
Prolegomena in Germany.

a systematic treatise on Christian doctrine, rather than a biblical theology in the sense in which the term was used on the
continent.[2] Curiously enough, the first original work in English
to deal with Old Testament theology seems to have been a
badly written and poorly printed volume called *Old Testament
Studies, an Outline of Old Testament Theology,* by Robert V.
Foster, professor in the theological school of Cumberland University, Lebanon, Tennessee. This work is a genuine treatise
on Old Testament theology and the author was quite familiar
with the previous history of the discipline, although the prove-
nance of the book clearly indicates its theological outlook.
Duff's *Old Testament Theology* published in Britain in 1891
is merely a history of the religion of Israel. The first real Old
Testament theology to appear in the British Isles was W. H.
Bennett's *The Theology of the Old Testament,* which was published in 1896 as one of a series of small theological textbooks.
The point of view is radically Wellhausian[3] and the theological
usefulness of the book is marred by the introduction of too
much purely archaeological information. The one extensive
work in English is A. B. Davidson's *The Theology of the Old
Testament* (1904). Unfortunately, like so many books in this
field, it is a posthumous volume and consists of a collection of
papers of decidedly unequal value from different periods of
the author's life. They have been artificially arranged by an
editor under the three traditional "theological" heads, although
Davidson himself had specifically repudiated such a method of
treating the subject.[4] The author says, in the introductory chapter, "We do not find a *theology* in the Old Testament; we find
a *religion* . . . Hence our subject really is the History of the

2. Cf. *supra,* p. 16.
3. The name of Moses is not even mentioned in the section devoted to
Israel's religious history!
4. A. B. Davidson, *The Theology of the Old Testament,* p. 13.

Religion of Israel." [5] The deficiencies of this one major English work on the subject serve to emphasize the slight attention which English-speaking scholars have given to this important branch of biblical studies in the past and the poverty of their contribution to it. Small as is its compass, C. F. Burney's *Outlines of Old Testament Theology* in the Oxford Church Text Books series (1904) is a far more satisfactory work and packs a great amount of significant information into a few (129) pages, although the material is presented with no especial breadth or depth. Mention should also be made of two other works which, without taking the name, deal in fact with Old Testament theology and are still widely used. These are H. W. Robinson's *The Religious Ideas of the Old Testament* (1913) and A. C. Knudson's *The Religious Teaching of the Old Testament* (1918). Robinson's work has considerably more philosophic depth than Knudson's and is on the whole a better book. Neither one, however, really attempts to present a unified view of the organic structure of Old Testament faith.

This completes the unimpressive list of works on Old Testament theology published in the English language before 1920. Perhaps there is something in the Anglo-Saxon temper averse to the kind of large-scale philosophic thinking required for the construction of a complete theology of the Old Testament; or it may be that the great age of biblical theology in English had not yet really begun.

5. *Ibid.,* p. 11; cf. p. 6.

VII

THE RENAISSANCE
OF OLD TESTAMENT THEOLOGY

The spiritual climate again became favorable to an interest in Old Testament theology in the two decades which followed the first World War. Several factors contributed toward this end: First was the general loss of faith in evolutionary naturalism, which resulted in a steadily increasing dissatisfaction with the religionsgeschichtlich attempt to explain Israel's religion as but one example of a universal law by which man inevitably progresses from animatism to ethical monotheism. Second, there was a reaction against the mid-nineteenth century conviction that historical truth can be attained by pure scientific "objectivity" or indeed that such objectivity is itself attainable. Stated in positive terms, there was a growing feeling that the inner truth of history, in contrast to mere external facts, is accessible only to those who in some way "feel themselves into" the situation which they are attempting to describe so that they in some sense become participants, not mere observers. This feeling manifested itself in an impatience with any mere "historicism" which does not concern itself with the significance and permanent value of the things with which it deals. Third, was the trend of continental theology back toward the Reformation— a trend which both rehabilitated the somewhat suspect term "theology" and gave a new impetus to biblical studies as being profoundly relevant to modern theological problems. All these tendencies helped to bring about a revival of interest in Old Testament theology, since this organic and systematic method of presenting Old Testament religion, in contrast to the mere History of the Religion of Israel, is by its nature chiefly concerned with the permanent, rather than with the accidental and temporary, elements in Israel's religion, and provides an account of the faith of ancient Israel which makes evident the relation of that faith, point by point, to modern theological needs.

The first work on Old Testament theology which appeared after the War, E. König's *Theologie des Alten Testaments* (1922), cannot, however, be regarded as a sign of the times. It is, rather, the last burst of an old fire than the kindling of a new. König, who published this work at the age of seventy-six, had written his first book before Wellhausen's *Prolegomena* appeared and during the intervening years had never faltered in his defense of an extremely conservative view of Israel's religious history. Nevertheless, it is true that König's views seemed less anachronistic in 1922 than in 1912 and his vigorous polemic against the pure religionsgeschichtlich method was certain to receive a more sympathetic hearing. He declared himself opposed to any method which exalts the evolutionary principle to a dogma and which carries the comparison of religions so far that *vergleichen* (to compare) becomes the equivalent of *ausgleichen* (to ignore differences).[1] He insists that the characteristic phenomena of Hebrew religion, such as prophecy, cannot be explained merely by genetic and psychological methods, but only as the product of "actual disclosures from beyond."[2] It should be noted that König, with all his conservatism, completely rejects all "spiritualizing" exegesis and insists upon the sole validity of historical-grammatical principles.[3] In the organization of the material, König follows a now familiar pattern by prefixing a general and historical section to a discussion of particular doctrines. His reconstruction of the history is almost painfully eccentric.

1. E. König, *Theologie des Alten Testaments,* p. 4.
2. *Ibid.,* p. 87.   3. *Ibid.,* p. 16.

König's book is largely significant as a curiosity. The real beginning of the renaissance of Old Testament theology is marked by an article published by C. Steuernagel in 1925[4] entitled "Alttestamentliche Theologie und alttestamentliche Religionsgeschichte." He pleaded for a renewed cultivation of the older discipline on these simple and practical grounds: First, scholars in other fields of study need some place to which they may turn in order to discover easily what the Old Testament has to say about the great topics with which all religions are concerned; second, the student of New Testament, or of dogmatic theology, has similar need of some place where he may learn the chief *results* of Old Testament studies as they bear upon religious doctrines; and, finally, there are elements in Old Testament religion which are essentially timeless and which can be more clearly presented by the method of topical discussion than by chronological arrangement.

Unfortunately, the subject of biblical theology in general became somewhat obscured at this period because of the tendency of some of the new dialectical theologians, especially in England and America, to use the term to describe their own theological systems—as supposedly being *based* upon the Bible in a sense in which other theologies are not. The subject became further confused because some of the newer theologians began also to rebel against historical-grammatical exegesis and to make use of "pneumatic," Christological, typological, and allegorical exegesis. As a result of these different tendencies, the term Old Testament theology has in recent times come to be used in at least two different senses: on the one hand, for a *systematic* and *unifying,* but strictly *historical* approach to the religion of the Old Testament, and, on the other, for a *theological* and *dogmatic* approach.

An excellent example of the latter use of the term is to be found in an article by Professor Eissfeldt entitled "Israelitisch-jüdische Religionsgeschichte und alttestamentliche Theolo-

4. In *ZAW*, Beiheft 41 (Martifestschrift), pp. 266-273.

gie" [5] in which he defends the conception that, in contrast to the historical-critical science called the History of the Religion of Israel, Old Testament theology has *religious faith* for its unique organ of knowledge, and only those elements in the Old Testament which can be regarded as Divine Revelation for its subject. It follows as a necessary conclusion (and one frankly accepted by the author) that anyone's Old Testament theology will be determined by the Church or sect to which he adheres. A conception more remote from Gabler's classic definition can hardly be imagined! This conception was directly challenged by Professor Eichrodt in an article published three years later[6] which strongly defended the traditional view of Old Testament theology as an empirical-historical discipline which is to be regarded as a branch of biblical science rather than of dogmatic theology. In contrast to the history of Israelite-Jewish religion, which is concerned with a genetic understanding of the Old Testament faith as it arose amidst the interplay of historical forces, Old Testament theology, he declared, is concerned with the great systematic task of making a *crosscut* (*Querschnitt*) through that religion in its classic form.[7]

In 1931 a work appeared which, though it did not bear the name, actually was a treatise on Old Testament theology. This was *Die Religion der Heiligkeit* by J. Hänel. He used the name *Ideengeschichte*[8] to describe his approach to the subject, partly no doubt because he was chiefly concerned to demonstrate that the *idea* of "holiness" [9] is the basic and unifying principle of Old Testament religion. He attempted to explain all the phenomena of Old Testament religion by appeal to this one concept. In the pursuit of his end, he professed to use purely em-

5. *ZAW*, 44 (1926), pp. 1-12.
6. "Hat die alttestamentliche Theologie noch selbständige Bedeutung innerhalb der alttestamentlichen Wissenschaft?" *ZAW*, 47 (1929), pp. 83-91.
7. *Ibid.*, p. 89.   8. J. Hänel, *Die Religion der Heiligkeit*, p. 55.
9. Defined as *"der absolute Abstand zwischen Gott und Mensch,"* ibid., p. iii.

pirical methods, but believed that at the end of such a task one might raise his "empirically obtained insight" into the world of authoritative value by a "pneumatic judgment"—one which would then be not *merely* "pneumatic," but would have a firm empirical basis.[10]

The ferment of thought in biblical and theological circles, to which the literature just mentioned gives testimony, was bound eventually to result in a conscious attempt to carry out once more the special task of Old Testament theology. The year 1933 marks the beginning of a period which may well be called in the future "the great age" of the discipline. In that year, Professor Eichrodt published the first volume of his truly monumental and epoch-making work and in the same year Ernst Sellin issued his two small volumes, *Israelitisch-jüdische Religionsgeschichte* and *Theologie des Alten Testaments*. Eichrodt's book will be discussed later. Sellin's books in no way compare with it either with respect to breadth or depth, since Sellin intended merely to provide a brief manual for the use of students. On the other hand, Sellin's views concerning the nature of the discipline are interesting and in some ways unique. He regards the two disciplines with which his volumes deal as organically related and would prefer to speak of them as one discipline which he would call "Old Testament theology upon a religious-historical foundation." [11] Both parts, he believes, are equally necessary. In harmony with his conviction that Old Testament theology is a "Christian-theological" as well as a historical discipline, he would limit its contents to those parts of the Old Testament which come to completion in the Gospel, though he admits that this is more easily said than done.[12] The material is arranged under the time-honored rubrics of God, Man, Judgment, and Salvation.

10. *Ibid.*, pp. 314 f.
11. E. Sellin, *Israelitisch-jüdische Religionsgeschichte*, pp. 1 f.
12. Sellin, *Theologie des Alten Testaments*, pp. 1 f.

The same outline is followed in L. Koehler's small *Theologie des Alten Testaments* published in 1936. This is a somewhat weightier book than Sellin's, but suffers badly from lack of proportion. Koehler would be willing to call any book a theology of the Old Testament which offers "a synthesis (*Zusammenstellung*) of such ideas, thoughts and concepts of the Old Testament as are, or could be, theologically important." [13] He finds the unifying idea of the Old Testament in the concept of God as the Lord (*Adon*) and of man as his obedient servant.[14] The entire treatise is based upon grammatical-historical interpretation and there is no evidence of the use of any kind of "spiritualizing" exegesis. Although Koehler plainly conceives his subject in terms of Christian theological study, yet the specific relation of the Old Testament to the Christian Scriptures appears only in a concluding rhetorical question, "In the New Testament stands the question, 'Do you understand what you read?' " [15]

The *Biblische Theologie des Alten Testaments* of Wilhelm and Hans Moeller (1938), though symptomatic of the general revival of interest in the subject, is an eccentric work, notable chiefly for its advocacy of the doctrine of "verbal inspiration" and its complete rejection of critical methods;[16] the whole being seasoned with a sinister touch of anti-Semitism.[17] The material is dealt with in terms of *Heilsgeschichte*.

Incomparably the greatest work ever to appear in the field of Old Testament theology, in terms both of sheer magnitude and of depth of insight, is Walther Eichrodt's *Theologie des Alten Testaments,* of which the first volume appeared in 1933, the last in 1939. In contrast to the books of Sellin and Koehler, this work is not a mere students' manual, but an original and exhaustive treatment of the whole subject. It is Eichrodt's posi-

13. L. Koehler, *Theologie des Alten Testaments,* p. v.
14. *Ibid.,* p. 12.   15. *Ibid.,* p. 230.
16. W. and H. Moeller, *Biblische Theologie des Alten Testaments,* pp. 4, 13 f.   17. *Ibid.,* p. 514.

tion that the religion of the Old Testament, in spite of all the changes which it experienced throughout its historical course, was a self-contained unity of constant basic tendency and type.[18] The task of Old Testament theology is to give a total picture of the world of Old Testament faith, a crosscut through the Old Testament world of thought, keeping always in mind its essential relationship to the religion of the larger Near Eastern world, as well as its special relation to the New Testament.[19] Although the article previously referred to[20] makes it clear that the method to be followed is the empirical-historical, yet Eichrodt also insists that the Old Testament cannot be understood apart from its relationship to the New, a relationship which is not merely preparatory, but is characterized by a real movement of life which passes between the two Testaments in both directions and which makes the Old Testament a permanent part of the Christian revelation.[21] The great fact which unites the two Testaments is that of the irruption (*Einbruch*) of God into his world in order to establish his kingly rule.[22] While Eichrodt feels the importance of knowing the History of the Religion of Israel, he does not agree with writers like Schultz and Sellin who feel that a historical section must be prefixed to any treatise on Old Testament theology. For Eichrodt, this is a subject which can be adequately dealt with in a general history of Israel.[23] He is strongly opposed to the use of the categories of dogmatic theology to provide an outline for the theology of the Old Testament, since they have grown up on entirely different soil and necessarily introduce a foreign element into the picture. The material must be arranged according to a pattern drawn from the dialectic of the Old Testament itself, which tells of a *national* God, who also shows himself to be the God of *the world* and of *individual* men. This leads Eichrodt to divide his treatise into three corresponding

---

18. W. Eichrodt, *Theologie des Alten Testaments,* I, Vorwort.
19. *Ibid.,* p. 2.   20. See *supra,* p. 64, n. 6.   21. Eichrodt, *op. cit.,* I, 1.
22. *Ibid.*   23. *Ibid.,* p. 5.

parts: God and Nation; God and World; God and Man.[24] The unifying "idea" of Old Testament religion he finds in the conception of *the Covenant*. This absorption in the idea of the Covenant and the arbitrary division of the material under the three heads just mentioned constitute the chief source of weakness in Eichrodt's book. The Old Testament faith cannot be naturally divided in this fashion and the attempt to do so leads to a considerable amount of wearisome repetition as well as the artificial separation of topics which properly belong together. The idea of the Covenant is far from omnipresent in Old Testament literature and only by a *tour de force* can it be made to appear so. Nevertheless, the book is an amazing achievement and it has already come to occupy a semi-authoritative position in the field which is not likely soon to be challenged. On the whole, the author is remarkably successful in giving a sympathetic picture of Old Testament religion as a unity, and is particularly to be honored for having done justice to the priestly as well as to the prophetic strain, showing them to be complementary rather than antagonistic elements in Israel's faith.

The year 1940 saw the publication of the *Theologie des Alten Testaments* of Paul Heinisch, a Dutch Roman Catholic and professor in the University of Nijmegen. Though more comprehensive than the books of Sellin and Koehler, it is intended, like theirs, to be primarily a students' handbook and consequently lacks the originality and philosophic depth of Eichrodt's three great volumes. It is admirably adapted to its purpose. Heinisch picturesquely describes his task to be that of gathering together the building stones which are scattered throughout the individual books of the Old Testament and from them to erect a building.[25] Although he had originally intended to prefix a historical introduction to his systematic treatment of the material, he found that considerations of space

24. *Ibid.*, p. 6.   25. P. Heinisch, *Theologie des Alten Testaments*, p. 5.

rendered that impossible. The major divisions of his book are: God; Creation; The Conduct of Life; The World Beyond; and Salvation. The great progress made in Roman Catholic biblical circles in recent times becomes startlingly evident when the critical and exegetical views represented by this book are compared with those of Hetzenauer, a generation earlier.[26] Except in certain crucial instances, Heinisch's interpretation of Old Testament religion does not differ greatly from that of modern Protestant scholarship; if only he had written after 1943, when the encyclical *Divino afflante spiritu* removed most of the restrictions under which Roman Catholic scholars had suffered since the beginning of the century, the *rapprochement* would have been even clearer. These facts are important as indicating the irenic function which can be served by the scientific study of biblical theology.

Certain other works which do not belong strictly to the field of Old Testament theology should be briefly noted here because of their collateral interest. J. Pedersen's *Israel, Its Life and Culture* (Vols. I-II, 1926; Vols. III-IV, 1940) is an important and highly original study of the psychology and thought-forms of the ancient Hebrews. Perhaps more than any other writer he has caught the peculiar quality of the Hebrew soul. Hempel's *Gebet und Frömmigkeit* (1922) and *Gott und Mensch* (1926) are important contributions to certain aspects of the same subject, as is his more recent *Das Ethos des Alten Testaments* (1938). Hempel finds the characteristic form of piety in the Old Testament to consist in the tension created by the sense of God's nearness (*Verbundenheitsgefühl*) and his remoteness (*Abstandsgefühl*). Similar to Hempel's books in subject matter is Baumgärtel's *Die Eigenart der alttestamentlichen Frömmigkeit* (1932). Wilhelm Vischer's *Das Christuszeugnis des Alten Testaments* (1934 and later) is a running theological commentary on the Old Testament,

26. See *supra*, p. 56, n. 18.

strongly influenced by the theology of Barth. The interests of this book are dogmatic rather than biblical-theological, but it provides a striking illustration of the renewal of interest in the theological significance of the Old Testament. Vischer believes that every word of the Old Testament points to Christ,[27] although he professes to reject "pneumatic exegesis." [28] Vischer stands rather in the line of such nineteenth-century biblicist theologians as Hofmann[29] than of the great writers on Old Testament theology such as Oehler and Schultz. The same is true of such English writers as A. G. Hebert[30] and W. J. T. Phythian-Adams, who have nevertheless done valiant service in arousing a greater interest in the objective theological content of the Old Testament (Old Testament theology proper) as well as in the use of Old Testament materials for the purpose of present-day theological reconstruction. In both England and America numerous articles dealing with the revival of Old Testament theology appeared in theological journals and a new periodical, *Interpretation,* was founded to deal with "the Bible and theology," in which many articles in the general field of Old Testament theology have already appeared. Old Testament scholars such as H. H. Rowley, R. B. Y. Scott, and G. Ernest Wright[31] published books dealing specifically with the religious, as opposed to the merely historical, literary, or archaeological values of the Old Testament, and two scholars, N. H. Snaith and H. W. Robinson, produced volumes which are at least essays in the direction of a real treatise on Old Testament theology. Snaith's *The Distinctive Ideas of the Old Testament* (1944) is a valuable essay on certain basic ideas in the Old Testament doctrine of God. H. W. Robinson had projected a complete treatise on Old Testament theology, but his untimely death prevented him from carrying out his pur-

27. W. Vischer, *Das Christuszeugnis des Alten Testaments,* I, 29.
28. *Ibid.,* p. 36.   29. See *supra,* p. 48.
30. In *The Throne of David* (1941). His *Authority of the Old Testament* is of somewhat different character.   31. See Bibliography B.

pose. Fortunately, he had at least published a preliminary sketch in the volume of essays entitled *Record and Revelation*[32] and the materials which he intended for an introduction to the completed work were posthumously published (1946) under the title *Inspiration and Revelation in the Old Testament.*

With so many published works appearing in the thirties and especially the late forties, after the end of the second World War, there could scarcely be any doubt that the renaissance of Old Testament theology, and of "biblical" theology in general, had become one of the most striking phenomena of the Christian theological world both on the continent of Europe and in English-speaking lands. By the middle of the century it seemed clear that this long-neglected discipline had at last come into its own and was on the verge of entering a golden age.

32. H. W. Robinson (Ed.), *Record and Revelation,* chap. v.

VIII

A GOLDEN AGE

A distinct turning point in the history of the discipline occurred in 1949. That year saw the publication of the first book
to appear in English under the title "Theology of the Old
Testament" since 1904, the date of Burney's and Davidson's
works.[1] The author was Otto J. Baab, a professor at Garrett
Biblical Institute, Evanston, Ill., who had previously published an article on the methodology of the subject.[2] Although
his book broke no new paths, it represented a competent re-
working of the traditional subject matter, illuminated by a
pervasive concern for the relevance of the Old Testament to
Christian theology and to life in the modern world. Baab understood the task of the Old Testament theologian to be that
of expounding, according to "logical principles derived from
his own scientific training," [3] "the religious consciousness of
the people" of Israel,[4] which is centered in a unique and con-
trolling experience of God. The framework he adopted was
essentially that of Man-God-Salvation, with the last division
extended by a series of chapters on Israel's understanding of
the Kingdom of God, and its approach to the problems of
death and evil. The book concludes with a discussion of the
permanent validity of the basic concepts of Old Testament

1. See *supra*, pp. 59 f.
2. See Bibliography B.
3. O. J. Baab, *The Theology of the Old Testament*, p. 21.
4. *Ibid.*, p. 20.

religion and a brief account of the relation of the Old Testament to the New.

The same year saw the publication, in Germany, of Otto Procksch's *Theologie des Alten Testaments*. Although it appeared after Procksch's death (which occurred in 1947), it is not, like so many other works in the field, strictly a posthumous work, since the author himself prepared the manuscript for the press and its appearance was delayed only by the advent of the War. Procksch acknowledges his deep indebtedness to J. C. K. Hofmann[5] for his understanding of history as the stage on which revelation takes place. Old Testament theology must be a "theology of history" (*Geschichtstheologie*).[6] The revelatory history with which it is concerned reaches its final fulfilment in the person of Christ.[7] Since, however, faith is required for understanding the significance of the revealing events, an Old Testament theology is possible only for those who share the biblical faith.[8] Unlike most others, Procksch does not wish to eliminate *Religionsgeschichte* entirely from the biblical-theological method, although he acknowledges that it can give only "esthetic," not "existential," insight into its subject matter. He proposes to integrate it into the total scheme as a first step, because Old Testament theology is concerned with historical revelation and makes use of historical categories of thought, and therefore needs to utilize the historical-chronological (*religionsgeschichtlich*) approach as well as the logical-systematic.[9] In accordance with this program, Procksch divides his book into two nearly equal parts: the first is concerned with the world of history (*Die Geschichtswelt*), the second with the world of thought (*Die Gedankenwelt*)—a pattern already familiar to us from the work of Schultz[10] and Sellin.[11] The second of these sections, the strictly biblical-theological, has

5. See *supra*, p. 48.
6. O. Procksch, *Theologie des Alten Testaments*, pp. 44 f.   7. *Ibid.*, p. 1.
8. *Ibid.*, pp. 14 f.   9. *Ibid.*, pp. 17-19.
10. See *supra*, p. 56.   11. See *supra*, p. 65.

a tripartite division which represents Procksch's most distinctive contribution to the methodology of the subject: I. God and the World; II. God and the Nation; and III. God and Man. It was from Procksch's lectures that Eichrodt had got the idea for the main divisions of his own work, which are identical except for the significant reversal in the order of the first two.[12] Procksch's book begins with the striking affirmation "all theology is Christology" but he makes no attempt to introduce this concept into the body of his work. The treatment of particular items is kept strictly on the level of scientific investigation.

The third book to appear in this important year 1949 was the Dutch scholar Th. C. Vriezen's *Hoofdlijnen der Theologie van het Oude Testament* (translated into German in 1956 and into English in 1958). Because the work was intended for the instruction of clergy and theological students rather than for other scholars, it is broader in conception and less technical than such works as those of Procksch and Eichrodt. The plan and treatment are admirable, the systematic part beginning with a chapter on "the knowledge of God" (which is taken to mean living in close relationship with him). There follow chapters dealing with God, Man, the intercourse between God and Man, ethics (intercourse between man and man), and the idea of the Kingdom of God. This is, of course, substantially the God-Man-Salvation outline, despite the author's explicit rejection of any attempt to press the material too neatly into such a scheme.[13] The most distinctive feature of the book is a long prefatory section, nearly a third of the total, devoted to the authority and value of the Old Testament, its use in the Church, its literary and spiritual content, and, finally, the principles and methodology of Old Testament theology. He denies the validity of Procksch's proposal to integrate *Religions-*

12. See *supra*, pp. 67 f.
13. Th. C. Vriezen, *An Outline of Old Testament Theology*, p. 124.

geschichte into the method, since the proper concern of a theology of the Old Testament is in no sense the religion of Israel in its historical development, but rather the canonical Old Testament itself. The Old Testament as a literary document stands as the final product of Israel's religious history and its contents are the deposit of a long process of selection and synthesis. Old Testament theology is concerned with the final result, not with the process.[14] The Old Testament theologian always has in mind the relevance of his subject matter to Christian theology, even when this is not in the forefront of his discussion.[15]

In 1950 Paul Heinisch's *Theologie des Alten Testaments,*[16] originally published in 1940, was translated into English, providing English-speaking Roman Catholics for the first time with a textbook of their own. The fact that it was published by the Liturgical Press (Benedictine Order) is indicative of the close relationship between biblical theology and the liturgical movement. This arises in part from a growing realization that ancient Israel was primarily a community organized for worship, and in part from an increasing recognition among biblical scholars that typology—the basic language of the Christian liturgy—has its roots in a characteristic mode of biblical (specifically Old Testament) thinking.[17] While Heinisch's book remains the only comprehensive Roman Catholic treatise on the theology of the Old Testament in English, other scholars of that communion have shown great interest in Old Testament studies and their theological significance. Father McKenzie's *The Two-Edged Sword,* for example, though by no means a work on Old Testament theology, contains a broad survey of certain elements of permanent value in ancient Hebrew thought, which touches upon many areas of biblical-theological concern.[18] For the French-speaking Catholic there are now

14. *Ibid.,* p. 121 (cf. pp. 14 ff. and pp. 40 ff.).   15. *Ibid.,* p. 124.
16. See *supra,* pp. 68 f.   17. See *infra,* pp. 94 f.   18. See Bibliography.

available two volumes of an exhaustive *Théologie de l'Ancien Testament* (1954, 1956) by P. van Imschoot. It is an elaborately documented work, systematizing the theological content of the Old Testament according to a pattern which keeps as close as possible to that of Christian dogmatic theology. Mention should also be made of two brief, elementary works by Father Albert Gelin: his *Key Concepts of the Old Testament,* translated into English in 1955, a simple book of orientation for the lay reader, and his *Religion of Israel* in the *Twentieth Century Encyclopedia of Catholicism* (1959).

The year 1950 also saw the inauguration of a new monograph series entitled *Studies in Biblical Theology.* By 1963 thirty-seven titles had appeared, twelve of them concerned with the Old Testament.

What many regard as the most satisfactory treatment of Old Testament theology for the clergyman or theological student who is not a specialist in Old Testament studies is the *Théologie de l'Ancien Testament* of Edmond Jacob, professor at Strasbourg, published in 1955 and translated into English in 1958. Similar in conception and bulk to Vriezen's book, some think it more useful because a larger portion of it is devoted to subject matter as contrasted with prolegomena (others, of course, think just the reverse!). Jacob, who has an attractive Gallic lucidity of style and little concern for theory, defines his goal in the opening sentence of the book as that of providing a "systematic account of the specific religious ideas which can be found throughout the Old Testament and which form its profound unity." He regards Old Testament theology as a historically-oriented discipline making use of the customary methods of scientific research. As a Christian theological discipline, it is necessarily concerned with the fulfilment of Old Testament history in Christ, and its conclusions should be valuable for understanding the New Testament and for the control of Christian dogmatic theology.[19] Its subject matter is not

19. E. Jacob, *Theology of the Old Testament,* p. 31.

institutions, ethics, or piety, but solely God—the affirmation of whose sovereignty is the unifying factor in Old Testament thought[20]—and God's relation to the world and man.[21] Although Jacob's conception of the subject is not especially different from that of many scholars who follow the traditional dogmatic-theological outline, he has preferred to arrange its various subdivisions under the following three heads: I. Aspects of God; II. The Action of God; III. Opposition to and Final Triumph of God's Work. This may not be a particularly happy outline, but it at least throws into strong relief the God-centered character of Jacob's discussion.

In 1959 another original work appeared in English, G. A. F. Knight's *A Christian Theology of the Old Testament*. The adjective "Christian" seems designed rather for the practical purpose of distinguishing the book from what had become a multitude of volumes with almost identical titles, than for indicating any radically new approach to the subject. All the works discussed hitherto have been by "Christians" who were well aware of the "Christian" theological significance of their studies. Knight, furthermore, in his introduction plainly repudiates the effort to understand the Old Testament "christologically." [22] In the body of his work he treats of substantially the same materials as the works previously discussed and, for the most part, in the same scientific spirit. Parts I, II, and III deal, respectively, with God, his Relation to the World, and with Israel; Part IV, entitled "The Zeal of the Lord" (more than a third of the book), treats of various aspects of the *Heilsgeschichte*. In this part alone homiletic interests tend sometimes to predominate over exegetical. Particularly dubious is the attempt to provide a schematic reconstruction of Israel's history with God in terms of a five-point "drama" consisting of: birth (Exodus), marriage (the Sinai Covenant),

20. *Ibid.*, p. 37.
21. *Ibid.*, p. 32.
22. G. A. F. Knight, *A Christian Theology of the Old Testament*, pp. 7 f.

death (Exile), resurrection (Return), and the *eschaton,* when God will finally assert his sovereignty and re-establish the harmony of the cosmos. The book is also marred at some points by the introduction of linguistic data which are, to say the least, dubious.[23] If, in many respects, this is a less satisfactory work than either Vriezen's or Jacob's, it nevertheless provides a useful supplement to theirs in the many paragraphs devoted to Old Testament "imagery," much of which is directly relevant to the New Testament. Knight's treatment of such picturesque figures as "the Vine," "Son of Man," "the Bride," "the Rock," "the Branch," "the Suffering Servant," is unique and invaluable.

The works discussed up to this point, however different the outlines they may follow, have all been concerned to present some kind of "crosscut" through the thought-world of Israel, to expound the "ideas" (or "doctrines") of the Old Testament about God and Man and their relation to each other. But the 1950's saw a vigorous reaction, led by Gerhard von Rad and his disciples, against this manner of presenting Old Testament theology. Taking up once more the line laid down by J. C. K. Hofmann and F. Delitzsch,[24] they insist that it should be concerned only with Israel's proclamation of God's actions in history, not with general ideas, piety, or the world of thought. In a series of articles and monographs beginning in 1936,[25] von Rad had become increasingly concerned with the problem of the method of Old Testament theology and in *"Das form-geschichtliche Problem des Hexateuch"* (1938) had attempted to provide his theoretical views with a firm scientific basis by demonstrating that the basic structure of the Hexateuch is that of a cultic confession of faith; in other words, that Israel's distinctive religious life was founded on a "creed," whose nuclear elements can readily be isolated. The creed asserted that God, by a series of saving acts, had delivered his people

23. See *infra*, p. 97.   24. See *supra*, p. 48.   25. See Bibliographies B and C.

and given them the promised land. To this simplest statement of faith were later added the "themes" of a covenant given at Sinai, promises given to the nation's ancestors, and, last of all, the elements of the primeval history now found in Gen. 1-11. Von Rad's mature view is that most of the Old Testament is a series of expansions of, or meditations on, this historical creed, and that the study of the creed in its original form and later transformations is the sole proper subject of a theology of the Old Testament. "The subject matter . . . is, of course, not the spiritual and moral world of Israel and the conditions of her soul in general, nor is it her world of faith, all of which can only be reconstructed by means of conclusions drawn from the documents: instead, it is simply Israel's own explicit assertions about Jahweh." [26] The publication of von Rad's two-volume *Theologie des Alten Testaments* (1957, 1960) had been eagerly awaited both by his partisans and his detractors. Each volume corresponds to a major division of the subject, as von Rad sees it. Volume I is concerned, in the main, with the "theology" found in the historical traditions (the Hexateuch and its component documents), though it also contains a series of awkwardly appended chapters which deal with the David-and-Zion theme found in the Deuteronomist's and Chronicler's histories as well as in some Psalms, with Israel's "response" as perceived in the Psalter, and with the rise of rationalism and skepticism evidenced in the Wisdom literature. A good deal of the normal subject matter of Old Testament theology turns up unexpectedly in these latter chapters, but common sense is likely to characterize the book as a whole as a study in the history of traditions rather than "theology" in any ordinarily accepted meaning of the term. Volume II deals with the prophets, who, according to von Rad's view, must be treated separately since for them the *Heilsgeschichte* was a closed story. Their gaze is turned toward the future where they see

26. G. von Rad, *Old Testament Theology*, I, 105.

the promises implicit in the old traditions about to be fulfilled in an unexpected and wonderful fashion. The crucial events of the past were no longer important in themselves, but had become "types" of future divine acts of grace and condescension. Von Rad had previously defended this "typological" understanding of Scripture,[27] and in his *Theology* uses it both for interpreting the prophets and for bringing the Old Testament into organic relation with the New.[28] No one would question the great service von Rad has done in emphasizing that Israel's religion is based upon the recognition of God's saving acts rather than upon the revelation of general propositions. But, while no future Old Testament theologian will be able to ignore the centrality of the kerygmatic element in his subject, it seems probable that von Rad's book, with its eccentric organization and one-sided emphases, will be more valued for its many contributions to other aspects of Old Testament science than as a satisfactory treatise on Old Testament theology.[29] The author has also been criticized for his skeptical attitude toward the actual historical value of the traditions upon which he lays so much "theological" stress. While this skepticism raises no particular problems for Old Testament theology as a purely descriptive science, serious difficulties begin to stir as soon as a question is raised as to the ontological validity or existential relevance of Old Testament faith.

In the English-speaking world, von Rad's general point of view, minus his historical skepticism, has found its chief exponent in G. Ernest Wright, whose *God Who Acts: Biblical Theology as Recital* (1952) initiated a discussion of the merits of kerygmatic vs. propositional theology which continues to the present time. This book undoubtedly helped to create a more favorable climate for hearing von Rad himself, when the

27. See Bibliography C.
28. G. von Rad, *Theologie des Alten Testaments,* II, 334, 377-380, 384 f.
29. See the discussion of von Rad in W. Eichrodt, *Theology of the Old Testament,* I, 512-520; also the extended review article on von Rad's *Theology* by J. Barr in *ET,* 73 (1962), 142-146.

English translation of his *Theologie* began to appear (Vol. I, 1962). Wright, however, takes a distinctly more moderate position than von Rad.

The increased interest of the English-speaking world in the subject of Old Testament theology, however conceived, is clearly evidenced by the translation during this later period of both Koehler's (1957) and Eichrodt's studies (Vol. I, 1961). In addition, original works in English were produced by two scholars representing a Fundamentalist view: E. J. Young's *The Study of Old Testament Theology Today* (1958) and J. B. Payne's *The Theology of the Older Testament* (1962). The latter distinguishes between the Old Testament, which is a body of literature, and the "older testament" which is that aspect of God's saving arrangement for mankind which was made known before the coming of Christ.[30] While the author's major interest is in the "saving arrangement" to which Scripture testifies, he has no doubt that the books themselves ("in the inspired autographs") are identical with revelation.[31] In the preface he states that the purpose of the Old Testament is to proclaim God's plan of redemption rather than to present a theoretical system of doctrine, but the main body of his work conforms to the traditional dogmatic scheme, with the fact of the "testament" as the unifying factor: Part I is preliminary; Part II discusses the nature and history of the testament (i.e., the Covenant); Part III is concerned with the doctrine of God ("the testator"); Part IV, with Man ("the heir"); and Parts V-VII, with the Plan of Salvation.

Although Old Testament theology in these years continued to be primarily a Christian-theological discipline, such Jewish scholars as Martin Buber, Abraham J. Heschel, and Will Herberg published books and articles which showed a profound concern with both the theological content and contemporary relevance of the ancient Scriptures of their faith.[32]

30. J. B. Payne, *The Theology of the Older Testament*, Preface. Cf. also p. 74, n. 14. 31. *Ibid.*, p. 17. 32. See Bibliography.

During this period there remained a considerable group of scholars opposed on principle to the whole project of biblical theology. Such men of an older generation as W. A. Irwin and the late R. H. Pfeiffer were vocal in their criticism, although Irwin, at least, recognized that the intentions of the biblical theologians were good, even if, on the whole, their methods were bad. Pfeiffer's posthumous work entitled *Religion in the Old Testament* expressed both by its title and content a thoroughly unreconstructed antipathy to any attempt at imposing a "theological" framework on the religion of Israel. Both men regarded the *religionsgeschichtlich* approach to the study of Hebrew religion as the safest, if not indeed the only valid, one. More recently, younger voices have also been heard in opposition to the biblical-theological movement. Most notable is that of James Barr who has criticized the method of biblical theology in a magazine article,[33] and, in his *Semantics of Biblical Language* (1961) and *Biblical Words for Time* (1962), offered a broad and searching critique of the use of linguistic phenomena in some biblical-theological works. In actual fact, these two treatises are concerned less with the kind of books under consideration in this essay than with such books as Pedersen's *Israel,* Boman's *Hebrew Thought Compared with Greek* (1954), Tresmontant's *Study of Hebrew Thought* (1956), and the various theological word-books edited by Kittel, Richardson (1950), and von Allmen (1954), none of which treat specifically of Old Testament theology, although they deal with matters distinctly relevant to it. Only Knight's *Christian Theology*[34] comes in for special censure. Nevertheless, it is evident that Barr looks with disfavor on many aspects of the biblical-theological project. Most of his detailed criticism is sound, though he tends to draw more sweeping conclusions than the evidence warrants and the frequent acerbity of his tone is regrettable.

33. See Bibliography C.   34. See *supra,* pp. 77 f.

This essay originally (in 1949) ended with the statement that "the crest of the wave is yet in the future." Considering the number of books, articles, and monographs on Old Testament theology and such related subjects as Old Testament hermeneutics, the unity of the Testaments, the relation of biblical to dogmatic theology, etc., which have appeared since that date, the statement cannot be allowed to stand. The appended bibliography is the best evidence that the crest is past. It still is true that "the great work on Old Testament theology in English has yet to be written." But so many books are now available, including such exhaustive and epoch-making works as those of Eichrodt and von Rad, that perhaps it never will be written. In any event it seems safe to suppose that the next decade or so will be a period of assimilation, self-criticism, and consolidation rather than of continued expansion. What seems quite certain is that the study of Old Testament theology will not soon again suffer the neglect that was its fate during the first third of the twentieth century.

PART II

THE NATURE AND METHOD
OF THE DISCIPLINE

IX

THE NATURE
OF OLD TESTAMENT THEOLOGY

*The Various Possible Meanings of the Term
Biblical Theology*

The term biblical theology is susceptible of various definitions, as has frequently been observed.[1] These definitions fall into two groups depending on which word in the phrase they emphasize. Thus biblical theology *might* mean either a biblical kind of *theology,* or the theological part of *biblical* studies. Taking the first alternative, the term "theology" in turn might mean various things. It could mean, loosely, all the subjects taught in the divinity school curriculum (in which case, *biblical* theology would be that part of the curriculum which is concerned with the Bible);[2] or it might mean the particular branch of theological study called systematic or dogmatic theology (in which case *biblical* theology would be primarily the study of proof-texts[3]); or "theology" might mean a particular system of theological doctrines (in which case *biblical* theology would presumably be a system of theological beliefs which professed to be based solely on the Bible).[4] Historically, these are all exceptional uses of the term, although in comparatively recent times, the last of them has gained considerable currency amongst so-called neo-orthodox theologians.[5]

In the nineteenth-century theological literature of Germany, where biblical theology arose and reached its full development,

1. Cf., *supra,* p. 15.   2. See *supra,* p. 15.   3. See *supra,* p. 18.
4. See *supra,* pp. 16, 17, 47, 58 f., 63.
5. It would make for clarity if the term "biblicism" or "biblicist theology," which was occasionally used to describe the point of view of Hofmann and his followers, could be revived in the present century.

the term rarely, if ever, occurs in any of the above-mentioned senses. To German scholarship it did not mean the biblical part of theological studies nor a biblically oriented theological system, but rather the theological part of biblical studies, i.e., that part of the study of the Bible which is concerned with its theological or religious ideas rather than with its political history, literature, or archaeology. The study of the Bible in the theological curriculum is divided among several disciplines. Among these are Biblical Introduction, Biblical Archaeology, Biblical History, Biblical Exegesis, and, since the time of Gabler,[6] Biblical Theology. It is in this context that biblical theology, in its historical sense, must be understood and discussed. The collocation of topics here given suggests, in itself, that biblical theology is primarily *a historical discipline,* as are the others associated with it, and it follows, incidentally, that its method must primarily be that of other historical sciences, viz., empirical and inductive. That this has been the conception of biblical theology which has predominated throughout its history should be evident from Part I of this study. With rare exceptions, the writers who have been mentioned there accept Gabler's definition as at least their starting point. When writers such as De Wette, Vatke, and Bruno Bauer introduced philosophical ideas into their works, it was not because they wished to redefine biblical theology, but because they believed their philosophy gave them a new principle for attaining historical "objectivity." Similarly, orthodox writers such as Steudel, Hävernick and Oehler believed their faith gave them an equally "objective" standard for interpreting the historical facts. All were agreed that the function of the biblical theologian is to *describe* the religious ideas (the "theology") which the Bible actually contains, not to erect a system of belief on a biblical foundation. Thus Schultz[7] says: "Systematic theology has to present in one harmonious whole the moral and religious con-

6. See *supra,* pp. 22 f.   7. H. Schultz, *Old Testament Theology,* I, 5.

sciousness of an evangelical Christian of the present day, as based on the completed development of the Bible and on the ecclesiastical history of Christendom resulting therefrom. Biblical theology has to show, from a purely historical standpoint, what were the doctrinal views and moral ideas which animated the leading spirits of our religion during the biblical period of its growth." This definition is implicit or explicit in practically every work on the subject published during the nineteenth century. Until comparatively recent times, at least in Germany, the term biblical theology was reserved for a specific biblical-historical discipline "which has for its task the presentation of the total theological and ethical content of the Bible" [8] and was not ordinarily used for a system of theological doctrines which professes to be based upon purely biblical principles. It is this conception which is still explicitly defended by Steuernagel [9] and Eichrodt [10] and is implicitly accepted in such contemporary works as those of Sellin and Koehler.

In present usage the term has sometimes acquired a new connotation. Eissfeldt,[11] for example, apparently takes biblical theology to mean the study of the Bible by a special theological method which is available only to those who have the gift of "faith," an endowment which he plainly distinguishes from the mere capacity for sympathetic understanding (*Sicheinfühlen*). The supernatural gift of faith provides the believer with a new "organ" of interpretation.[12] Regardless of the merits of this position in itself (and it is a recurrent one), there is no historical reason for associating it with the term biblical theology, which actually, as we have seen, arose out of a revolt against what seemed to the eighteenth-century rationalists the perversion of the plain historical and grammatical sense of the Bible by the use of theological criteria.

8. Fr. Tossetti in the *Lexicon für Theologie und Kirche* (R. C.), II, 339 f.
9. See *supra,* p. 63.   10. See *supra,* p. 64.   11. See *supra,* pp. 63 f.
12. In this Eissfeldt is associating himself with the views of Procksch, whom he quotes approvingly. See *supra,* p. 73.

A Defense of the Traditional Use of the Term Biblical Theology

The only definition of biblical theology which does justice to the history of the discipline is that it is *the study of the religious ideas of the Bible in their historical context.*[13] However, it is not enough to show that only this use of the term is historically correct; it is also necessary to show that it continues to be the most useful. The following considerations seem to indicate that this is so: first of all is the fact that it is generally desirable to use words in senses which are already commonly accepted rather than to redefine them in unusual ways. Much confusion in contemporary writing on the subject would be avoided if biblical theology had not become so Protean a term. A second practical consideration is the difficulty of defining it in any other terms than those we have indicated. If it is used to mean a system of theology based upon the Bible, then it becomes a party term—a shibboleth—and, as such, belongs rather to the realm of polemics than of scholarship. If it is used to indicate the study of the Bible by a special theological method, then, by that very fact, it becomes indefinable, since even the nature of this method cannot be communicated to those who do not possess it. Biblical theology in this sense becomes an esoteric mystery rather than a science. Eissfeldt admits as much when he implies that there will be as many Old Testament theologies as there are creeds or churches.[14] This point of view seems to involve a kind of solipsistic irrationalism which precludes intellectual discussion. A third argument in favor of continuing to use the term in its traditional sense is the negative one that it is actually impossible to construct a

13. This is, of course, a merely minimum definition which will be amplified later.

14. O. Eissfeldt, "Israelitisch-jüdische Religionsgeschichte . . . ," *loc. cit.*

biblical theology in the sense of a system of belief which is based upon biblical principles and concepts alone. Every theological system which does more than repeat the phrases of Scripture makes use of selection and interpretation and is influenced by subjective attitudes from which no theologian can escape. The twentieth-century theologian can no more ignore his own mind and background than he can the long centuries of creative Christian thought and experience which lie behind him. It is important that he should remain as close to the Bible as possible and to this end there is no more useful tool than biblical theology in its traditional sense, but his own theological system can never be purely "biblical." It will be the resultant of at least three factors: the theology of the Bible; the long experience of the Christian community; and the way in which his own mind appropriates these facts and interprets them in relation to the needs and thought-forms of his own day. A fourth line of defense for the use of the term biblical theology as the name of a historical discipline will become evident in the next chapter, in which we shall consider the services such a discipline is able to render to other branches of the organism of theological studies, and in the final chapter, in which we shall consider the positive contributions it can make to contemporary theological thinking.

"Old Testament Theology" Distinguished from "The History of the Religion of Israel"

Having established in general the character of biblical theology as a historical science, it is now necessary to establish a criterion for distinguishing biblical theology from the History of Biblical Religion,[15] or, to speak in terms of our present concern, Old Testament theology from the History of the Religion of Israel.

15. The definition given on p. 90 would obviously cover both.

As we have seen, the two disciplines were not distinguished until the end of the nineteenth-century,[16] but were regarded rather as two alternative methods which could be used within the framework of a single discipline called "The Biblical Theology of the Old Testament." Since that time they have been clearly differentiated and the distinction has been chiefly based upon the difference in their methods of dealing with the material. One treats of the story of Israel's development in its chronological sequence; the other describes the persistent and distinctive principles of Old Testament religion in some kind of logical or "theological" order. This distinction is described by Eichrodt[17] in terms of the difference between a "lengthwise section" and a "cross section" (*Querschnitt*). It is sometimes suggested that there is a further essential distinction between the two disciplines, viz., that the History of the Religion of Israel is coldly objective and "scientific" in its handling of the material while Old Testament theology deals with the material as *Revelation* and seeks to determine its relevance to Christian theology and to the contemporary scene. This distinction is not entirely without justification, but that it does not belong to the essential *differentiae* is shown by the fact that the first biblical theologies[18] were strictly objective and even adversely critical in their attitude toward the material; that such later biblical theologians of the first rank as Schultz, König, and Eichrodt insist upon maintaining an attitude of scientific objectivity (so far as it is obtainable in any historical science); and that Histories of the Religion of Israel have been written, such as those of König, Kittel,[19] and Sellin, which are as profoundly concerned with the religious and theological importance of the matter with which they deal as any book on "Old Testament theology." If the History of the Religion of Israel has normally

16. See *supra*, pp. 50 ff.   17. In the article referred to *supra*, p. 64, n. 6.
18. See *supra*, pp. 24 ff.
19. R. Kittel, *The Religion of the People of Israel*, English trans. (1925), especially see p. 223.

been characterized by impartiality and disinterestedness, that is largely due to the fact that it first came into being as a theological discipline under the influence of the religionsgeschichtlich school, whereas Old Testament theology rather remained the special preserve of more conservative students of the Bible. Fundamentally, there is no reason why this should be so. Unless the History of the Religion of Israel is to be transferred from the faculty of Christian Theology to that of the History of Religions, we must certainly agree with Sellin[20] that this discipline, too, must deal with the Old Testament as Revelation and be concerned with the theological significance of its subject-matter. The chief intellectual currents of the day—the reaction against barren historicism and the demand for spiritual commitment—leave no place in the theological curriculum for any discipline which is not concerned with the discovery and propagation of *Christian* truth.

Since, then, both the History of the Religion of Israel and Old Testament theology, in varying degrees, make use of historical methods and may both have a specific theological orientation, it seems proper to reaffirm the conclusion previously reached, that the *essential* distinction between them lies in the difference between the chronological and the systematic approach, the difference between the "long-cut" and the "cross-cut."

Alternative Names for Biblical (or Old Testament) Theology

The name of the discipline has been variously framed. Some[21] have preferred to call it "biblical dogmatics." This is objectionable because the Bible actually contains no "dogmas" and, furthermore, the term seems to exclude such matters as

20. E. Sellin, *Israelitisch-jüdische Religionsgeschichte*, I, 1.
21. De Wette and Lutz.

ethics and piety which properly belong within the general field. Knapp alone calls it *Biblische Glaubenslehre;* Dillmann tentatively suggests the name *Biblische Religionslehre;*[22] Hänel calls it *Ideengeschichte;*[23] Sellin uses the mouth-filling phrase "Old Testament theology on a religious-historical foundation." [24] None of these terms have commended themselves to a wider circle. One might perhaps regard "the theology of the Old Testament" as a more accurate term for the present purpose than "Old Testament theology" and attempt some kind of distinction between them. Historically, though, the terms have been used interchangeably and it is hardly likely that any distinction can be introduced at this late date. It is important, however, to observe that the full title of our discipline in Germany has always been "the biblical theology of the Old Testament." This points to the fact that "Old Testament theology" must be seen as related to a larger context. While in theory it might have originated in Judaism or amongst scholars with no religious convictions, it did in fact originate in the Christian theological curriculum and has always been regarded as part of the larger discipline called "biblical theology." Therefore, by history and definition, Old Testament theology is *a Christian-theological discipline* and, as such, does not deal with the Old Testament in isolation, but always has some concern for its relation to the New.

Conclusion: Basic Definition of "Old Testament Theology"

To sum up, one may provisionally define "the biblical theology of the Old Testament" (more briefly, "Old Testament theology") as that Christian theological discipline which treats of the religious ideas of the Old Testament *systematically*, i.e.,

22. A. Dillmann, *Handbuch der alttestamentlichen Theologie*, p. 1.
23. See *supra*, p. 64.   24. See *supra*, p. 65.

not from the point of view of historical development, but from that of the structural unity of Old Testament religion, and which gives due regard to the historical and ideological relationship of that religion to the religion of the New Testament. This definition, it should be noted, is still merely basic and descriptive. The following sections will amplify it, and in the final section,[25] a definition of more normative character will be attempted.

25. See *infra*, p. 122.

X

THE FUNCTION
OF OLD TESTAMENT THEOLOGY

The Organic Interrelatedness
of the Theological Sciences

In order to understand the nature of Old Testament theology, it is necessary not only to define it, but to determine the function it is intended to perform as part of the total organism of theological studies. The four broad fields into which the theological curriculum is divided—the Biblical, Historical, Dogmatic, and Practical—are not simply a congeries of ill-assorted and unrelated subjects, but have a definite relationship to each other, each contributing to or receiving from the others. It is this flow of life and inspiration from the one to the other which justifies our calling the theological curriculum an "organism." The ultimate purpose of the whole is twofold: to prepare men for the Christian ministry, and to contribute by study, research, lecture, and publication to the general enlightenment of the Christian community with regard to the faith by which it lives. It is our immediate purpose to describe the position occupied by Old Testament theology (as a branch of the larger discipline of biblical theology) within this organism and to determine the contribution it may be expected to make toward the final purposes for which the organism exists.

Old Testament Theology as the Crown
of the Old Testament Sciences

If Old Testament theology is, as has been previously maintained,[1] one of the Old Testament sciences rather than a part

1. See *supra*, pp. 87 ff.

of dogmatic theology, then it must be the crown of them all, since the construction of a scientific theology of the Old Testament presupposes the results of all the other Old Testament studies and also because these varied studies require some further study to collate and synthesize their results so as to make them available to other branches of theological science and to the world of secular learning as well.[2] This is explicitly stated by many writers on the subject.[3] No one would be qualified to deal with Old Testament theology who had not previously mastered in some degree all the subjects in the Old Testament field. The task, indeed, is so enormous that few have ever felt qualified for it and it is this which has led to Old Testament theology's becoming largely "a science of posthumous works."

But if Old Testament theology is the crown of Old Testament sciences, it seems evident that its function cannot be *merely* descriptive. Here, more than any other place, it is necessary for Old Testament studies to be concerned with the value of the things with which they deal and to indicate their significance for the rest of life. Such concerns have their legitimate and necessary place in every aspect of Old Testament science, but, in the very nature of things, it will be in a special sense part of the function of this culminating study in the Old Testament field to deal with those things in Old Testament religion which are of permanent importance. Out of the mass of statistical, linguistic, and merely archaeological data which

2. A number of writers on the subject have pointed out that Old Testament theology not only receives from the other Old Testament sciences, but also reacts upon them. This is especially true of exegesis, since Old Testament theology provides it with that larger background of thought against which individual passages must be seen and thus helps to preserve the profound truth which underlies the old hermeneutical principle of *analogia fidei* (or *scripturae*), viz., that the correct interpretation of a passage involves at least in part its relationship to the larger whole.

3. e.g., E. Riehm, *Alttestamentliche Theologie*, p. 3; W. Eichrodt, *Theologie des Alten Testaments*, I, 1; A. Dillmann, *Handbuch der alttestamentlichen Theologie*, p. 5; C. Steuernagel, "Alttestamentliche Theologie und alttestamentliche Religionsgeschichte," *loc. cit.*

lie at its command, it will set forth with especial emphasis not only that which is most characteristic, but that which is of enduring worth. It must be stressed once again, however, that, in this respect, the distinction between Old Testament theology and other Old Testament sciences is not one of kind, but of degree and emphasis.

Old Testament Theology as a Propaedeutic for New Testament Studies

Within the larger area of biblical theology, Old Testament theology occupies a special position as a preparatory exercise for the study of the New Testament. Probably its greatest single function is to describe the thought-world out of which the New Testament grew. Scholars such as Schleiermacher[4] and Harnack[5] could regard the rise of Christianity within the world of Jewish culture as a mere historical accident which had no bearing upon the essential character of the Christian Gospel, but the present scholarly world has reacted strongly against this position and insists that, important as Persian, Hellenistic, and other elements may have been, the decisive influences are to be found in the Jewish, and especially the Old Testament, world.[6] New Testament religion is even more closely related to the Old Testament than to later Judaism and cannot be correctly understood without a knowledge of the Old Testament thought-forms which it presupposes. To men of the New Testament, as well as for those who hold the Christian faith today, this connection is not a merely external

4. F. E. D. Schleiermacher, *The Christian Faith,* English trans. (1928), pp. 60-62.

5. A. Harnack, *What Is Christianity?* English trans. (1904), pp. 164 f.; cf. the quotation in W. Vischer, *Das Christuszeugnis des Alten Testaments,* I, 30 f.

6. e.g., N. H. Snaith, *The Distinctive Ideas of the Old Testament,* pp. 9, 184 f.; W. F. Lofthouse, in *Record and Revelation,* pp. 459 ff.

one, as though Old Testament studies had something of the same kind of importance for New Testament science as the study of ancient history or Near Eastern culture. For Christian faith the connection of the Old Testament with the New is integral and organic so that the two together form an indissoluble unity, the one being the necessary completion and fulfillment of the other. Since Old Testament theology is a Christian-theological discipline, this conviction must be given due weight and serious consideration, although it does not necessarily lie within the province of Old Testament theology as such to determine the precise relationship of the Old Testament to the New.[7]

At this point, it will perhaps be helpful to give examples of areas in which the theology of the New Testament is specifically dependent upon that of the Old. Where the New Testament is silent on certain matters, it assumes that the teaching of the Old Testament is still valid. Jesus did not come to destroy, but to fulfill, the Law and the prophets,[8] and it seems self-evident that one cannot hope to understand Jesus or his first interpreters unless one first of all understands the Law and the prophets.

Illustration (1): The New Testament Doctrine of God Based on That of the Old. From the time of Marcion, it has been common to contrast the God of the New Testament with the God of the Old, as though the one were merely a God of wrath and justice, and the other a God merely of love and beneficence. This is not, of course, the point of view of the New Testament itself. Its God is explicitly "the God of Abraham, Isaac, and Jacob." [9] The New Testament, it is true, gives special emphasis to the gentler attributes of God, but these by themselves do not constitute a doctrine of God and, taken out of their Old Testament framework, can easily lead to theo-

---

7. This task rather belongs to the field of biblical theology as a whole.
8. Matt. 5:17.   9. Matt. 22:32.

logical sentimentalism. To understand the God of Christ or of Paul, one must first understand the God of Genesis I, of the Psalms, and the Second Isaiah. The Old Testament provides the solid background against which the New Testament doctrine of God must always be seen; indeed there is no New Testament doctrine of God apart from the Old, for the one includes, presupposes, and is built upon the other. It is from the Old Testament especially that we learn of God's work in creation, providence, and history, of his Personality and Uniqueness, his Power and his Glory, his Spirit and his Wisdom, and of the Justice, Holiness, and Goodness of his Character. It is one of the important services of Old Testament theology to describe and expound these things.

Illustration (2): "The Kingdom of God" Essentially an Old Testament Idea. The phrase "the Kingdom of God" is everywhere assumed in the New Testament to be of self-evident meaning.[10] It could be so only to one who was familiar with the use of the concept (if not the precise phrase) in the Old Testament, as it is found for example in the prophets and in Psalms 95-99. It is true that there are certain intermediate steps in the postcanonical literature which must be studied in order to understand the course of development from the one Testament to the other, yet the relationship is close and essential, and it might well be that New Testament scholarship would profit by devoting more attention on this point to a study of Old Testament theology and less to that of the obscure and ephemeral literature of the Apocalyptists.

Illustration (3): Old Testament Piety Basic to That of the New. Schultz makes the important observation that a pagan had really to be *converted* to Christianity, while the Jew who became a Christian could still remain a pious Jew.[11] This is because the type of piety created by the Old Testament and

10. e.g., Mark 1:15.
11. H. Schultz, *Old Testament Theology*, I, 51 f.

represented in its psalms, prayers, sermons, and confessional literature, remains essentially unchanged in the New. For this reason such studies as those of Hempel and Pedersen[12] are of great value, not only for an understanding of Israel's religion, but for the spiritual milieu of the Gospels.

These three illustrations are intended merely to suggest the importance of the contribution which Old Testament theology has to make to New Testament studies. Any attempt to develop them further would take us beyond the limits of the present discussion. The field itself is almost unlimited when one considers the bearing of the Old Testament upon such things, among others, as Eschatology, the Future Life, the Doctrine of Man, Personal and Social Ethics, the Doctrine of the Church, and the relation of the Church to the secular order.

Old Testament Theology as the Point of Departure for Historical Theology

Beyond the biblical sciences, Old Testament theology also has important functions to perform, although from this point on we must speak chiefly of biblical theology in general, since the larger discipline is the connecting link between Old Testament theology and the other theological disciplines. Nevertheless, it should be remembered throughout the following discussion that our principal interest is still in *Old* Testament theology. It has been pointed out by many writers[13] that biblical theology might be considered to be *the first chapter in the history of dogma,* and Old Testament theology the first long section of that chapter. The one essential qualification which

12. See *supra,* p. 69.
13. e.g., D. G. C. von Cölln, *Biblische Theologie,* p. 6; H. A. C. Hävernick, *Vorlesungen über die Theologie des Alten Testaments,* p. 2; Schultz, *op. cit.,* pp. 7 f.

must be added to this statement is that since biblical theology deals with the period which is normative for faith, there is also a qualitative difference between it and the later chapters.

Biblical (Old Testament) Theology in Relation to Systematic Theology

Far more important than this relationship to historical theology is the relationship of biblical theology to systematic or dogmatic theology. Historically, as we have noted, the term biblical theology first appears in connection with systematic theology, first as a means of supporting it, and later in reaction against it.[14] Even after biblical theology became legitimated as one of the biblical disciplines, under Gabler, it never ceased to have significance for the discipline which fathered it. Gabler himself regarded it as one of the important functions of biblical theology to provide a sound *basis* on which a dogmatic theology could be erected,[15] and later writers for the most part agree.

(1) Biblical Theology Provides the Basic Materials for Systematic Theology. Systematic theology draws for its materials upon natural theology and upon the experience of the Christian community, but its primary source is the Bible; otherwise it would cease to be in any distinctive sense *Christian* theology. The best way to obtain these materials is by a comprehensive study of the religious conceptions of the Bible as a whole such as is offered by biblical theology rather than by obtaining mere fragments of doctrine through a study of classic proof-texts or favorite passages. The special study of Old Testament theology will contribute certain basic emphases without which the structure of Christian theology would be notably weakened.

(2) Biblical Theology Provides a Norm for Systematic

14. See *supra*, pp. 18 ff.
15. See *supra*, pp. 22 f.

Theology. The second function which biblical theology as a whole can perform in relation to systematic theology is that of providing a norm by which later theological developments may be judged.[16] Systematic theology is by no means identical with biblical theology, but it needs to be continually compared with it so that its own false or eccentric emphases may be corrected. Biblical theology provides a pattern which indicates the contours and true proportions of the Christian faith. The study of biblical theology can do much to keep a sense of balance and proportion in theological thinking and keep it from straying into dangerous subjectivism. The present demand for a more "biblical" theology is, of course, rooted in part in a feeling that the liberal theology which arose out of German philosophical idealism had become unduly subjective and had lost its roots in historic Christianity. The analysis was accurate, but in some respects the cure has been as bad as the disease, for the new "biblical" theology has often seized on certain striking but isolated ideas in biblical religion and constructed its system upon them. The best antidote for both the disease and the cure is the discipline *properly* called biblical theology, which endeavors to set forth the total religious thought-world of the Bible and thus to present all particular ideas in the larger context in which they belong and in which alone they are valid.

The Relationship of Biblical (Old Testament) Theology to Practical Theology

In the past, biblical theology has been regarded too narrowly as something of value only to scholars. Riehm was almost unique in recognizing that one of its primary purposes must be to assist in "the building of the Kingdom of God." [17] There

16. Cf. Dillmann, *op. cit.,* pp. 5-7; Schultz, *op. cit.,* pp. 4-7.
17. See *supra*, p. 52.

are two practical areas in which it can be especially useful: First of all, it can be of great value to the minister in the preparation of his sermons. Since it endeavors to picture the whole sweep of biblical religion, it can help him to preach from the Bible as a whole, and not to concentrate upon a small collection of "great texts." It will mediate to him the most recent results of critical and archaeological scholarship in terms of their significance for contemporary religious thought. It will assist in giving greater variety to his preaching and save him from subjectivism and narrow preoccupation with a few well-worn themes. Furthermore, it will help him to interpret individual texts with greater accurateness since it presents the background of thought against which they should be interpreted.[18] In the second place, the study of biblical theology should be an instrument for the cultivation of personal piety, especially amongst the clergy. The excessive atomism of much modern biblical study has so tended to reduce the Bible to fragments that a sense of the unity and meaning of the whole has largely been lost. As a result, the inspiration which used to be derived from biblical study has often disappeared. Biblical theology helps to correct this by presenting the organic structure of biblical religion in all its towering strength and grandeur. This means, of course, that if it is to fulfill its purpose, biblical theology will not be content merely to *describe,* but will also seek to *communicate.* There will be scope for the use of the disciplined imagination, aesthetic appreciation, and literary art. Any account of the religion of the Bible (or, specifically, of the Old Testament) which properly fulfills its function will necessarily enlarge and deepen the spiritual vision of those who study it.[19]

18. Cf. *supra,* p. 97, n. 2.

19. The present writer has attempted to give practical expression to the ideal described in this paragraph in his *Design of the Scriptures: A First Reader in Biblical Theology* (1961).

XI

THE SCOPE
OF OLD TESTAMENT THEOLOGY

Two questions arise with regard to the scope of the discipline: Should it make use of sources outside the canonical Old Testament? And, to what extent should it attempt to deal with *all* the Old Testament material?

Old Testament Theology Should Properly Be Limited to the Canonical Books

Most of the early writers[1] and some of the later[2] include the so-called intertestamental literature within the scope of Old Testament theology. Most later writers, however, tend to limit it more sharply to the canonical writings[3] or to use material outside the canon only for the elucidation of special points,[4] or to show how particular Old Testament doctrines such as those concerning angels and the Resurrection later developed and finally assumed the form in which we find them in the New Testament period.[5] In actual fact, the inclusion of any *comprehensive* attempt to deal with the intertestamental literature[6] in Old Testament theology quite obviously weakens the artistic unity of the presentation, as can be seen by an examination of those Old Testament theologies which endeavor to do so.

1. e.g., G. L. Bauer, De Wette, von Cölln, Steudel.
2. König, Sellin.   3. Oehler, Schultz.   4. Heinisch.
5. W. Eichrodt, *Theologie des Alten Testaments,* I, 6.
6. More especially the rabbinical writings, Josephus, and the Pseudepigrapha.

The proper place in which to deal with such material is in a separate discipline, which has been called variously "Introduction to New Testament Theology" [7] and "History of the New Testament Period." [8] Treated in this fashion, it becomes a prelude rather than an anticlimax. There is a freshness and creativity about the material contained in the canonical Hebrew Old Testament which is not to be found in the later productions of the Hebrew genius and the impact of which should not be diminished by the inclusion of a literature which is at best derivative, and at worst is largely contaminated by foreign influences.

Old Testament Theology Should Deal Only with the Distinctive and Characteristic Religious Ideas of the Old Testament

(1) It Should Exclude Mere Archaeological Information. Oehler is the chief apologist for the view that Old Testament theology should include all the material in the Old Testament which bears upon religion.[9] His own book is the best argument against this theory, since it is so laden with merely archaeological information that it becomes more of a dictionary of the Bible than a book of "theology." Most writers sharply distinguish between biblical theology and biblical archaeology, using the latter term in the old-fashioned sense to designate information which has largely an antiquarian interest, while biblical theology is concerned solely with such things as directly concern Israel's faith and world-view. This distinction commends itself to an age in which one of the chief complaints is the undue proportion of attention which biblical science has paid to history, literature, and archaeology as distinguished from

7. H. Schultz, *Alttestamentliche Theologie,* p. 60.
8. Eichrodt, *loc. cit.*
9. G. F. Oehler, *Prolegomena,* p. 6; Oehler, *Old Testament Theology,* p. 6.

faith. The renewed interest in Old Testament theology largely springs from a desire to escape the dominance of the merely antiquarian. While the line of demarcation is not always easy to draw, the general rule will be that nothing should be included in Old Testament theology which is not directly relevant to an understanding of the living faith of the men of ancient Israel. There is no need, for example, to go into such matters as the details of the sacrificial cultus or the pre-Hebrew origins of cultic objects and acts.

(2) Its Primary Concern Should Be with Ideas, Not with History or Institutions. Should Old Testament theology to any extent include Old Testament history? It was Oehler's contention that it should, since he conceived of the Old Testament revelation as consisting of a series of divine acts in history rather than in the communication of ideas.[10] In other words, he believed that the Hebrew people had no theology other than the facts of their history. Oehler by no means excluded all the intellectual element from his account of the religion of Israel, but some other writers such as Moeller[11] and the biblicist theologians of the type of Hofmann[12] apparently reduce Old Testament theology to Heilsgeschichte, so that it consists of almost nothing more than the history of the religious experience of Israel. This differs from Old Testament Religionsgeschichte in that it pictures that history entirely in terms of "the mighty acts of God" rather than of a purely natural evolution. Important as the idea of Heilsgeschichte is, and valid as may be the view of revelation in the Old Testament which it embodies, it certainly does not correspond to what has historically been called Old Testament theology and there seems

10. See *supra,* p. 44.   11. See *supra,* p. 66.
12. See *supra,* p. 48. Cf. also the views of von Rad and Wright, *supra,* pp. 78-81. While the present writer has prefixed a section on "History" (*Heilsgeschichte*) to the section on doctrine in his *Design of the Scriptures,* he would doubt that this is necessary or practical in a work dealing only with Old Testament theology.

to be no reason for confusing issues by allowing it to appropriate that name. There is a legitimate place for both Religionsgeschichte and Heilsgeschichte, but there is also a useful place for the discipline called Old Testament theology. While the religious ideas of the Old Testament do not, for the most part, appear in theological form, there is a *theology* in the Old Testament in the sense of a structural complex of ideas which are logically dependent upon the central idea of God, and it has been the historic task of Old Testament theology to explore that structure of thought and expound it. Many of the religious ideas of Israel have been mediated through its history, but they are still *ideas* and it is with these ideas that Old Testament theology has primarily to deal.

(3) Its Concern Should Be the Normative Religion of the Old Testament. Thus far we have narrowed the materials of Old Testament theology to those which give expression to *religious ideas* or attitudes. We must now determine whether, without further discrimination, it includes in its synoptic view *all* such views and attitudes as the Old Testament itself contains. The early rationalistic writers[13] gave a positive answer to this question and indeed were inclined to emphasize unduly the primitive "folk-religious" elements in the Old Testament in order to show the superiority of the Gospel. De Wette, however, already made a distinction and included in his biblical dogmatics only such doctrines as agreed with "rational faith." [14] Most later writers accept some such limitation.[15] Since it has become the special function of the History of the Religion of Israel to deal with the total phenomena of Hebrew religion and to show the evolution, if such there be, of higher ideas from lower, there would seem to be hardly any question

13. Such as Bauer and Kaiser.
14. W. M. L. De Wette, *Biblische Dogmatik der Alten und Neuen Testaments,* p. 31.
15. e.g., F. Hitzig, *Vorlesungen über die biblischen Theologie des Alten Testaments,* p. 3; P. Heinisch, *Theologie des Alten Testaments,* p. 1.

that the proper subject of Old Testament theology should be what might be called *"normative* Old Testament religion." Proper scientific procedure demands that the criteria for determining what belongs to that normative religion and what does not should be derived from the Old Testament itself and not imported from outside, either in the form of De Wette's rationalism or Sellin's limitation of the discipline to those ideas which are presupposed by the New Testament. One must honestly face the Old Testament on its own ground and try to discover what were the essential elements in the religious world-view which was actually current in Israel during her great creative period. The Old Testament theologian will make use of merely popular religion and superstitions only insofar as they seem to him in some way to illuminate the basic inner core of Israel's faith. Two standards are of primary importance in determining what this normative religion is: The first is that of *persistence* or *pervasiveness,* i.e., that the particular views under consideration are found in every period and, to a greater or less degree, seem to be assumed by all the Old Testament writers. The second standard is that of *distinctiveness.* There are certain ideas which are that rare and final flowering of the Hebrew spirit, such as are found, for example, in Isaiah 53 or Jeremiah 31:31 ff. These would be excluded by the first rule, but must be included in the scope of the discipline because without them we should miss the purest distillation of Old Testament faith.

(4) It Should Include All the Major Tendencies of Normative Hebrew Religion. Subjective considerations have led most writers on Old Testament theology to stress one of the three main streams—prophetic, priestly, and sapiential—which make up Old Testament religion, and to neglect the others. The older orthodoxy, as exemplified by Oehler, tended to over-emphasize the priestly; the Wellhausen School has always been inclined to overvalue the prophetic and to regard the priestly

as no part of the legitimate religion of Israel. Almost all have regarded the Wisdom Literature as a foreign element. Even amongst recent writers on the subject,[16] the tendency remains to treat the prophetic element as alone normative and to regard the priestly as a pathological excrescence. Such an evaluation of the priestly tradition in Israel is obviously not the result of an attempt to enter sympathetically and without prejudice into the total thought-world of the Old Testament, nor does it do justice to the sources. It is one of the great merits of Eichrodt's book that he can deal with the priestly point of view and exhibit it as complementary rather than antagonistic to the prophetic.[17] No writer on Old Testament theology has the right arbitrarily to exclude either the priestly or prophetic material from the scope of the discipline, since neither is really intelligible, or capable of maintaining itself, without the other. The priestly element is the bony skeleton of the religion whereas the prophetic is the living flesh which clothes it. The Wisdom strain is a more difficult one to deal with, but it occupies too prominent a place in Old Testament literature to be simply disregarded. Here, too, the Old Testament theologian has the duty of attempting to enter sympathetically into this world of reflective and speculative thought and trying to discover whether or not it has an organic relation to the other strains.

(5) It Should Include a General Discussion of Ethical Principles. All writers on the subject discuss the question whether Old Testament theology should include a treatment of Hebrew ethics. De Wette and Lutz rigidly excluded it and therefore justified their use of the term biblical dogmatics instead of biblical theology. Oehler, at the opposite extreme, included the whole subject. Steudel took a mediating position,

16. e.g., L. Koehler, *Theologie des Alten Testaments,* pp. vi, 170.

17. e.g., Eichrodt, *Theologie des Alten Testaments,* I, 41. See also G. von Rad, *Old Testament Theology,* I, 260; E. Jacob, *Theology of the Old Testament,* pp. 262 f.; Th. C. Vriezen, *An Outline of Old Testament Theology,* p. 280.

and proposed to include ethics only in so far "as the essential elements of the ethical consciousness are connected with the forming of the relationship between man and God." [18] This is the position taken by most of the later writers[19] and seems a sound one. Ethics and religion are connected so uniquely and indissolubly in the Old Testament that a discipline which pretends to deal with the religious consciousness of Israel must perforce give some account of ethical principles and show their vital interrelatedness to "doctrine," but an exhaustive treatment of the details of Old Testament law and ethics would require a disproportionate amount of space and is better reserved for special study.

(6) It Should Include a Discussion of the Nature of Hebrew Piety. It remains to raise the question whether Old Testament theology should properly include a study of what today might be called "the religious psychology" of the Hebrews. De Wette[20] and von Cölln[21] both explicitly include this aspect (*Gefühlsstimmung*), but it has not played a large role in the later history of the discipline. This indeed is a major criticism which might be directed against most of the classic works on the subject. They deal with the religious ideas of Israel only from the outside and but rarely give the reader a sense of the deep feeling and the profound moods of piety which gave warmth to the ideas. Such works as those of Hempel and Pedersen[22] have a large contribution to make to this phase of the subject. It is one of the great merits of Eichrodt's work that it includes a great deal of this element. At the same time, his book illustrates the danger involved in attempting to delve into the mental patterns of others, since often, especially in the third volume, where this kind of discussion most largely

---

18. J. C. F. Steudel, *Vorlesungen über die Theologie des Alten Testaments,* p. 74.
19. e.g., Heinisch, *op. cit.,* p. v.   20. See *supra,* pp. 29 f.
21. D. G. C. von Cölln, *Biblische Theologie,* p. 5.
22. See *supra,* p. 69.

appears, Eichrodt's psychological reconstruction is either too subjective or too elaborate to be entirely convincing. Too great an interest in this aspect of the subject can lead a writer into the kind of amorphousness which characterizes Riehm's book[23] or the irritating subjectivism of Ewald.[24] It is all too easy to confuse one's own subjectivity with that of the ancient Hebrews. Nevertheless the task is an important one and should not be neglected.[25] Much of the renewed interest in biblical theology today is based upon a feeling that biblical studies have been too much concerned with external details and have entered too little into the spirit and moods which produced the Bible. Biblical studies have dealt more than adequately with the facts, but have failed to communicate the underlying life. It is part of the task of Old Testament theology to rectify this error.[26]

23. See *supra*, p. 52.

24. See *supra*, pp. 47 f.

25. Jacob rejects both ethics and piety from the subject matter of his book. See *supra*, pp. 76 f. Von Rad excludes them by definition (*supra*, p. 78), but includes an excellent account of the mood of worship in his chapter "Israel Before Jahweh," *op. cit.*, pp. 356-370. Vriezen includes both piety and ethics, *op. cit.*, pp. 301-342. J. Muilenburg has an excellent little book, *The Way of Israel* (1961), in which faith, piety, and ethics are blended in a harmonious and satisfying mixture.

26. The question might be raised in this connection whether the term "religion" might not better be substituted for "theology" in the name of the discipline. The writer would reject this suggestion on the ground that the term "religion" is either (in the psychological sense) too vague and subjective or (in the religionsgeschichtlich sense) too broad and comprehensive, and also that it does too little justice to the structural character of Old Testament faith. The "religion" of the Old Testament is the *expression* of its "theology," as every high religion is an expression of some kind of theology.

XII

THE METHOD
OF OLD TESTAMENT THEOLOGY

Since the general question of the method of Old Testament
theology is so extensive as to require a special treatment by
itself, we shall here be content with attempting to answer two
questions only: What method of interpreting the biblical material is to be used? And, under what clear and logical rubrics
can the results be arranged?

The Approach to Old Testament Theology

(1) Old Testament Theology Uses Historical and Critical
Methods Alone. We have already rejected the suggestion that
biblical theology is to be *defined* by reference to its use of some
special "theological" method.[1] The question still remains
whether it may *make use* of such a "theological" method as
one of its tools. The historical section of this study will have
made it clear that the biblical theologians of the past have, with
almost complete unanimity, rejected any such suggestion. In its
essence, biblical theology, as defined from Gabler's day on, has
been a science which attempted to deal with a historical question in a historical spirit, which does not mean, of course,
coldly and impersonally. The discipline so defined has played
an important role in the organism of theological sciences in the
past, and, as the writer has tried to show, has an equally important role to play today. Any modification of its character

1. See *supra*, pp. 88 f.

which would remove it from the realm of historical studies and assign to it special methods inaccessible to other historical sciences would seriously impair its usefulness in playing this role. However appealing may be some of the arguments in its favor, any so-called special "theological" method is a dangerous expedient which opens the door for the unlimited play of subjective ideas and theological prejudices, and which can only cause the general conclusions of the science to be viewed by others with gravest suspicion. A second, and even more important, consideration is the fact that the Christian faith is rooted in history. So far from its being true that a scientific and historical approach to the Bible involves a repudiation of the Christian world-view in favor of a modern, and suspect, "historicism," the very historical character of the Faith itself implies that we should endeavor to understand the Bible on the historical level and let it speak to us in its own language. This is the task of biblical theology and that task should not be made impossible by permitting it to use a special method which removes its conclusions from the realm of scientific control and which opens the way for every interpreter to impose his own ideas upon it. The Bible, whether its origin be human or divine, is a fact of history and should be reverently and seriously dealt with as such. Therefore Old Testament theology should make use of grammatical-historical methods of interpretation alone to the exclusion of allegorical, typical, or "pneumatic" exegesis. The *primary* function of the Old Testament theologian is not to answer the question, "What does the Old Testament mean to me or to my sect?" but, "What did the religious concepts found in the Old Testament mean to the men of Old Testament times?"

(2) The Method of Old Testament Theology Involves a Need for Sympathy and Insight. Must the Old Testament theologian then adopt a "purely objective attitude" to his material? If by "purely objective" one means an effort to interpret

historical facts honestly, accompanied by a sincere effort not to read one's own ideas back into a historical situation, then the answer is "Yes." But if one means a cold, external, disinterested, and impersonal attitude, the answer is emphatically "No," simply because no historiographer can adequately discharge his task in this fashion. The present reaction against "historicism" is, in part, a reaction against the belief that the ideal approach to history is to be found in the kind of external subject-object relationship to the material which prevails in the physical sciences. The objective of all good historical writing is not mere chronography, but the imaginative re-creation of the stream of history with all its richness of human life and feeling—a re-creation which can hardly fail to show, in the very telling, the relevance of the past to the present. This can only be accomplished as the writer who deals with the events, ideas, or institutions of the past approaches them with sympathy and insight. Today, the biblical theologian who is conscious of the meaning of his task must not be afraid to acknowledge the legitimate place his own subjectivity must play in this, *as in all historical studies*. Eichrodt, in the same article in which he defends the view that Old Testament theology is a part of empirical-historical biblical science,[2] also points out the role that must be played by the subjective in all attempts to write even contemporary history. It will be evident in the selection of material, the choice of leading ideas (*Leitgedanken*), and in the adoption of a particular perspective. While the historian should endeavor to eliminate all mere prejudice and *Tendenz* from his work, he should not lament the existence of subjectivity, since it is only the presence of his own personality in the process which makes it possible for him to clothe the subject with flesh and blood. There must be, Eichrodt says, a spontaneous act of creation, a release of the powers of the soul, by which one takes the historical truth up into himself

2. See *supra*, p. 64.

and *then* reproduces it. Schultz had already said much the same thing: "It is self-evident that biblical theology can be a profitable study only to one who is able to bring himself into living sympathy with the spirit of that religion. No spiritual movement can or will reveal itself in all its truth except to one who, having come under its charm, keenly appreciates its real meaning, and takes an interest in all its peculiar characteristics." [3] Thus the scientific historical method which is proper to biblical theology should involve that sympathy and insight, that sense of personal participation, which is indispensable to all good historical study. The revolution which has taken place in recent years in the theory of historiography should do much to deepen and enrich the study of Old Testament theology.

(3) Faith Helps to Make Such Insight Possible. In theory, it is hard to see how one could maintain that religious faith is any more essential for the study of Old Testament theology than for studying the history of Christian dogma. In fact, though, it is difficult to see how one could write sympathetically of the theology of the Old Testament who did not in some way share the Old Testament faith. Indeed, it is also difficult to believe that one could really write satisfactorily of the history of the Church or of dogma who did not share the Church's faith sufficiently to be able to realize that a controversy over *homo-ousion* and *homoi-ousion* might involve something more serious than the quality of a vowel. In all the history of the discipline, only Kaiser[4] has attempted to write a biblical theology without professing to hold the biblical faith, and none has failed more abjectly in understanding the character of biblical religion. His work was a *tour de force* which is not likely to be repeated. We may assume that the Old Testament theologian of today, at least, will be a man of faith, who, with all his adherence to critical and historical methods, is seeking to learn about something which is of vital concern to himself.

3. H. Schultz, *Old Testament Theology*, I, 11.   4. See *supra*, pp. 28 f.

Eichrodt[5] makes the point that, while the Old Testament theologian is under no obligation continually to be making existential judgments, yet his work is begun under the presupposition of an existential judgment. It may be taken for granted that this is true, and if so, it will be of great advantage to him in the accomplishment of his task, not because he is thereby endowed with a miraculous new organ for the attainment of knowledge, but simply because it puts him *within* the stream of which the Old Testament is a part and makes possible that inner sympathy with his subject which, as we have seen above, is essential to all good historical writing.

The Organization of Old Testament Theology

(1) The Question of a Unifying Principle. No question is more vexing to writers on Old Testament theology than the practical one of arranging its materials systematically and logically when there is scarcely a trace of such system and logic in the Old Testament itself. The early biblical theologians, for the most part, simply made use of the outline which they had inherited from systematic theology, distributing their materials under the general headings: Doctrine of God, of Man, and of Salvation; and the majority even of later writers have continued to make use of some variant of this scheme. Others, however, feeling the danger of imposing an outline derived from another discipline upon the biblical materials, have sought to derive some principle of organization from the Old Testament itself. One favorite device has been to find some single unifying principle around which the material could easily be arranged. De Wette was the first to advocate this procedure.[6] Like Vatke, Bruno Bauer, and Hitzig after him, he stated this principle in philosophical terms. Later writers stick

5. In the article referred to previously. See *supra,* p. 64, n. 6.
6. See *supra,* p. 30.

more closely to the Bible. Schultz (like Baumgarten-Crusius) found the unifying principle in the conception of "the Kingdom of God," i.e., in "the fact that the perfect spiritual God wishes in love to realize His holy will in communion with man." [7] Dillmann[8] and Hänel [9] found it in the idea of God as "the Holy." Eichrodt finds it in the conception of "the Covenant" [10] and Koehler[11] in the conception of God as "Lord" (*Adon*). None of these principles works out as well in practice as in theory and all lead either to a forcing of the material into a bed of Procrustes to fit the theory or a tacit disregard of the theory when the application becomes difficult. Eichrodt frequently does the former by introducing his favorite idea of the Covenant in contexts in which neither the word nor the idea occurs;[12] Schultz takes the latter, and probably safer, course by actually arranging his material in accordance with common sense rather than according to his "principle." The fact is that the choice of any one such unifying principle does violence to Old Testament religion and cannot be justified from the sources. The center of Old Testament religion is really to be found in its doctrine of God with all its richness and variety, not in any neat formulas such as those given above, or in the popular stereotype of "ethical monotheism." Eichrodt unconsciously acknowledges this fact when, following Procksch's example, he names his three volumes, *Gott und Volk, Gott und Welt, Gott und Mensch.* It is largely this centrality of the doctrine of God which justifies us in speaking of an Old Testament *theo*-logy. Certainly we do not use the term in the sense

7. H. Schultz, *Old Testament Theology,* I, 56.
8. A. Dillmann, *Handbuch der alttestamentlichen Theologie,* p. 27.
9. See *supra,* p. 64.
10. W. Eichrodt, *Theologie des Alten Testaments,* I, 6.
11. L. Koehler, *Theologie des Alten Testaments,* p. 12.
12. Cf. *supra,* p. 68. In a review in *Theologische Rundschau* (1935), Koehler unkindly remarks that the prophets would no doubt have had more to say about the Covenant if they had had the advantage of reading Eichrodt's book!

of a closely articulated system of doctrine, but of a complex of religious ideas which center in certain basic ideas about God—who he is and what he does. It is the centrality of the idea of God which gives to the Old Testament that structural and organic unity which it is the task of Old Testament theology to describe and discuss.[12a]

(2) What General Rubrics Should Old Testament Theology Use? Very early there arose the shibboleth that Old Testament theology should be organized according to a method which would arise from the materials themselves, rather than one imposed from the outside.[13] The majority of writers in the field have been content to use the traditional "theological" heads with some modification and elaboration, but others[14] have either written Heilsgeschichte or like Eichrodt adopted some unusual and complicated system which they believed to conform better to the nature of the material. The fact is that any method of arrangement we may adopt will be one imposed from the outside. Despite Ewald,[15] nothing was more foreign to Israel's genius than the idea of systematic organization. Consequently, we are forced to seek for some method of organization which (1) will be simple, and (2) will present the material in a form meaningful to *us*. For this purpose it seems difficult to think of a better outline than that which is used by systematic theology, since this outline arose from an attempt to answer the basic questions concerning human life: What is the nature of God in his perfection? (theology); what

12a. Jacob, most recently, has declared his adherence to this view. See *supra*, p. 77. Baab makes "experience of God" central (*supra*, p. 72); Vriezen, "the knowledge of God" (*supra*, p. 74).

13. See Zachariae, *supra*, p. 21; W. M. L. De Wette, *Biblische Dogmatik der Alten und Neuen Testaments*, pp. 38 f.; D. G. C. von *Cölln, Biblische Theologie*, p. 33; H. A. C. Hävernick, *Vorlesungen über die Theologie des Alten Testaments*, p. 3; Eichrodt, *Theologie des Alten Testaments*, I, 5.

14. Moeller and, in part, Oehler; most recently von Rad (*supra*, pp. 78-81). See also *supra*, p. 107.

15. See *supra*, p. 47.

is the nature of man in his weakness? (anthropology); what is
the nature of that dynamic process by which man's weakness
becomes reconciled with God's perfection? (soteriology). This
is the kind of outline for which G. L. Bauer argued when
Old Testament theology was in its infancy,[16] and the kind
which has been used by the majority of writers down to our
own time, most recently by Sellin, Koehler, and (with some
elaboration) by Heinisch. This simple and obvious basic outline in no way distorts the material on which it is imposed,
and has the obvious advantage of making clear the relevance
of Old Testament religion to contemporary thought, since the
questions it seeks to answer for the religion of Israel are those
which are asked always and everywhere, questions which have
arisen not in the scholar's study or the lecture hall, but out of
man's existential situation.

Two Additional Questions

Two additional questions may be briefly referred to here.
The *first* is this: Is it necessary or desirable to follow the procedure used by Steudel, Dillmann, Schultz, and others, and
strongly advocated by Sellin[17] and Procksch,[18] of prefixing
a history of the religion of Israel to a systematic treatise on
Old Testament theology? While such a study is obviously a
prerequisite to the study of Old Testament theology, practical
considerations seem to indicate that it is better not to include it
in the scope of the discipline. The chief reason for this is that
the scope of Old Testament theology itself already is too vast to
justify expanding it still further by the inclusion of a historical
section. Heinisch[19] found this to be true in actual practice,
and Eichrodt managed to fill three volumes with a purely
systematic discussion. A further consideration is that it is

16. See *supra*, pp. 26 f.   17. See *supra*, p. 65.
18. See *supra*, p. 73.   19. See *supra*, pp. 68 f.

probably more useful and illuminating for the average student to study the history of Israel's religion in connection with her general history than to deal with it as an isolated subject or as a mere preface to Old Testament theology.[20] The *second* question is: Does a discussion of the nature of revelation and the present authority of the Bible properly belong within the scope of the discipline? The answer must be in the negative, since this question, being theoretical rather than historical, lies distinctly within the province of dogmatic theology and, though related to biblical theology, is not an integral part of it. This point of view will be reinforced by a study of those volumes on biblical theology which do endeavor to include it. Invariably this section is the weakest and least convincing part of such works and the one which possesses least permanent value, since it is inevitably less biblical than the other parts and more marked with the idiosyncrasies of its author and the age to which he belonged. This does not mean, of course, that the discipline should avoid a discussion of the ideas of revelation which are set forth in the Bible itself and the authority which such revelation had for men of the biblical period. Obviously, also, the biblical theologian has the *right* to discuss the present meaning of revelation and the authority of the Bible if he wishes to, since it is one of the most important subjects confronting contemporary theology, but he should be conscious that he does so, not in his capacity of biblical theologian, but in his capacity as a believer in, and apologist for, the Christian faith.[21]

20. Cf. Eichrodt, *Theologie des Alten Testaments,* I, 5.
21. Vriezen has done this more successfully than most. See *supra,* pp. 74 f.

XIII

CONCLUSION

Final Definition of Old Testament Theology

In a previous section,[1] Old Testament theology was defined, descriptively, as "that Christian theological discipline which treats of the religious ideas of the Old Testament *systematically*, i.e, not from the point of view of the historical development, but from that of the structural unity of Old Testament religion, and which gives due regard to the historical and ideological relationship of that religion to the religion of the New Testament." On the basis of the discussion which has followed, but rearranging our conclusions in a form better suited to the logic of definition, we should now add: that (in our view) its scope should be, not the sum-total of religious phenomena in Israel, but rather the ideas and concepts of the normative or distinctive religion taught or assumed by the canonical books of the Old Testament, all of which have their center in a distinctive doctrine of God (theo-logy); that it should include broadly the subjects of ethics and cultus so far as these are expressions of distinctive religious ideas, but should specifically exclude mere antiquarian information about laws and religious customs; that it should aim, not merely to give a description of the religious ideas of Israel, but to com-

1. See *supra*, pp. 94 f. It should be emphasized that the adjective "Christian" is included here only because, as a matter of simple historical fact, Old Testament theology originated within the Christian theological curriculum. There is no theoretical reason why Jewish scholars should not also cultivate a biblical theology (although, for obvious reasons, it would not be called "Old Testament" theology).

municate in a vivid and moving way the piety which clothed those ideas with life and color. We should also add that its method is historical and critical, but like all other historical studies, demands sympathy, insight, and inner participation from the student, and that an invaluable precondition for such inner participation is that the student of Old Testament theology should in some sense share the Old Testament faith— to the extent that that faith continues to form a part of the Christian religious consciousness. Finally we should observe that it is the function of Old Testament theology to act as the culminating discipline of the Old Testament sciences and to constitute a bridge over which the most significant conclusions of technical studies in Old Testament Introduction, History, and Exegesis pass to become useful materials for the biblical theology of the New Testament and for Historical, Systematic, and Practical Theology.

Present Value of the Discipline

With respect to present-day theological tendencies, the study of Old Testament theology can have certain definitely salutary effects. In the first place, it will assist in combating the unfortunate effects of *undue fragmentation of biblical studies* and will help to restore that sense of the unity of the Old Testament and of the whole of Scripture which has been lost by an exaggerated emphasis upon the minutiae of exegesis and upon source and form criticism. It will help to show that the Bible has a significance as a whole and that its values are not confined to a few favorite passages. In the second place, it will help to restore the balance which has been lost by *the increasing secularization of biblical studies,* which have tended to put the major emphasis upon the linguistic, archaeological, and cultural-historical aspects of Old Testament science, and will tend to recall the attention of the scholarly world to that which is central in the Old Testament and which alone justifies the amount of time and energy spent in studying it, viz., its religious world-view. In the third place, the study of Old Testament theology will help to restore a sense for *the values which have been lost in modern liberal Christian theology,* particularly in regard to its tendency to denature and sentimentalize the character of God and to place too high a valuation upon the goodness and perfectibility of man. The transcendent Holiness of God, his Majesty, Power, and Righteousness are emphases of Old Testament religion which are also permanent elements within the general outline of Christian theology, and the study of Old Testament theology is a way of maintaining an accurate perspective with regard to these things. The same is true of the Old Testament view of man, which regards him as in constant need of repentance and imposes upon him a sense of dependence upon Divine help. The study of Old Testament theology is also the best way of bringing into sharp relief the Christian convictions that history, not the speculative intellect, is the principal locus of divine revelation, and that salvation is not offered to men individually but within the context of a saving community, Israel or the Church. In the fourth place, since Old Testament theology is a historical-critical science, in which the student endeavors to avoid reading his own prejudices into the material, but rather attempts "to see it steadily and see it *whole,*" it will also help to correct *the excesses of certain contemporary "biblicist" theologies* which seize upon particular aspects of Old Testament religion, such as the Wrath of God, the Idea of Judgment, and the Fallen Nature of Man and, by isolating them from their larger context, actually give a false impression of the character of the God of the Old Testament and of the characteristic moods of Hebrew piety. Old Testament theology takes into account not only the more frenetic utterances of the Hebrew prophets, but also the tender piety of the "Songs of Ascents," the vision of

God as the Lord of Nature in Genesis I and Psalm 104, the sacramental approach to God of the priestly code, the speculative and almost rationalistic approach of the Book of Proverbs, and the concentration upon God's grace and love found in Deuteronomy and Psalm 103. Old Testament theology, as a historical-critical discipline, is able to give all the elements of Old Testament religion in their true setting and relationship to each other and thus help to maintain a proper balance in modern theological thought as the latter quite rightly seeks to renew its vitality by drawing more deeply from the springs of biblical religion.[2]

2. There is a valuable discussion of the practical importance of the Old Testament for Christian theology in Godfrey E. Phillips' *The Old Testament in the World Church* (London, 1944).

ABBREVIATIONS

ATR   *Anglican Theological Review*
CBQ   *Catholic Biblical Quarterly*
CJT   *Canadian Journal of Theology*
CQR   *Church Quarterly Review*
ET   *Expository Times*
EvT   *Evangelische Theologie*
HJ   *Hibbert Journal*
Int   *Interpretation*
JBL   *Journal of Biblical Literature*
JBR   *Journal of Bible and Religion*
JR   *Journal of Religion*
JTS   *Journal of Theological Studies*
KD   *Kerygma und Dogma*
RL   *Religion in Life*
SJT   *Scottish Journal of Theology*
Theo   *Theology*
TL   *Theologische Literaturzeitung*
TZ   *Theologische Zeitschrift* (Basel)
VT   *Vetus Testamentum*
ZAW   *Zeitschrift für die alttestamentliche Wissenschaft*
ZTK   *Zeitschrift für Theologie und Kirche*

BIBLIOGRAPHY

A. "Biblical Theology" Before 1787

BAHRDT, KARL FRIEDRICH: *Versuch eines biblischen Systemes der Dogmatik.* Gotha and Leipzig, 1769.

BAIER, JOHANN WILHELM: *Analysis et vindicatio illustrium S. S. dictorum.* Altdorf, 1719.

BÜSCHING, ANTON FRIEDRICH: *Diss. inaug. exhibens epitomen theologiae e solis literis sacris concinnatae.* Göttingen, 1756.

—— *Epitome theologiae e solis literis sacris concinnatae, una cum specimine theologiae problematicae.* Lemgoviae, 1757.

—— *Gedanken von der Beschaffenheit und dem Vorzüge der bibl.-dogm. Theologie vor der Scholastischen.* 1758.

COCCEIUS, JOHANNES: *Summa doctrinae de foedere et testamentis Dei.* 1648.

CRUSIUS, C. A.: *Hypomnemata ad theologiam propheticam.* Leipzig, 1764.

GABLER, JOHANN PHILIPP: *Oratio de iusto discrimine theologiae biblicae et dogmaticae regundisque recte utriusque finibus.* Altdorf, 1787. Included in his *Opuscula Academica,* 2, 179-198. Ulm, 1831.

HAYMANN, CARL: *Biblische Theologie.* Leipzig, 1768.

HOFFMANN, JOHANN GEORG: *Oratio de theologiae biblicae praestantiae.* Altdorf, 1770.

HUFNAGEL, WILHELM FRIEDRICH: *Handbuch der biblischen Theologie.* Erlangen, Vol. 1, 1785; Vol. 2, 1789.

HÜLSEMANN, JOHANN: *Vindiciae S. S. per loca classica systematis theologici.* In his *Opuscula Academica.* Leipzig, 1679.

KÖNIG, GEORG: *Vindiciae Sacrae.* Nuremberg, 1651.

SCHMID, SEBASTIAN: *Collegium biblicum prius, in quo dicta V. T., et collegium biblicum posterius, in dicta N. T. iuxta seriem locorum communium theologicorum explicantur.* Strassburg, 1671.

TELLER, WILHELM ABRAHAM: *Topice sacrae scripturae.* Leipzig, 1761.

WEISSMANN, CHRISTIAN EBERHARD: *Institutiones theologiae exegetico-dogmaticae.* Tübingen, 1739.

ZACHARIAE, GOTTHILF TRAUGOTT: *Biblische Theologie.* Göttingen, 1772-75.

ZICKLER, FRIEDRICH SAMUEL: *Ausführliche Erklärung der Beweissprüche der heiligen Schrift in der dogmatischen Gottesgelahrheit.* Jena, 1753-65.

B. Old Testament Theology 1787-1949

ALEXANDER, W. LINDSAY: *A System of Biblical Theology,* ed. by J. Ross. Edinburgh, 1888.

AMMON, CHRISTOPH FRIEDRICH: *Entwurf einer reinen biblischen Theologie.* Erlangen, 1792; 2nd ed. 1801.

BAAB, O. J.: "Old Testament Theology, Its Possibility and Methodology," *The Study of the Bible, Today and Tomorrow,* ed. by H. R. Willoughby. Chicago, 1947.

BAUER, BRUNO: *Die Religion des Alten Testaments in der geschichtlichen Entwickelung ihrer Principien.* Berlin, 1838-39.

BAUER, GEORGE LORENZ: *Theologie des Alten Testaments oder Abriss der religiösen Begriffe der alten Hebräer von den ältesten Zeiten bis auf den Anfang der christlichen Epoche.* Leipzig, 1796.

——— *Dicta classica V. T. notis perpetuis illustrata.* Leipzig, 1798.

——— *Beilagen zur Theologie des Alten Testaments, enthaltend die Begriffe von Gott und Vorsehung, nach den verschiedenen Büchern und Zeitperioden entwickelt.* Leipzig, 1801.

——— *Hebräische Mythologie des Alten und Neuen Testaments.* Leipzig, 1802.

——— *Biblischen Moral des Alten Testaments.* Leipzig, 1803.

BAUMGÄRTEL, FRIEDRICH: *Die Eigenart der alttestamentlichen Frömmigkeit.* Schwerin, 1932.

BAUMGARTEN-CRUSIUS, LUDWIG FRIEDRICH OTTO: *Grundzüge der biblischen Theologie.* Jena, 1828.

BENNETT, W. H.: *The Theology of the Old Testament.* London, 1896.

BRIGGS, CHARLES AUGUSTUS: "Biblical Theology," *Biblical Study* (New York, 1891), 367-405.

BURNEY, C. F.: *Outlines of Old Testament Theology.* New York, 1904.

BURROWS, MILLAR: "The Task of Biblical Theology," *JBR,* 14 (1946), 13-15.

————— *An Outline of Biblical Theology.* Philadelphia, 1946.

CÖLLN, DANIEL GEORG CONRAD VON: *Biblische Theologie.* Leipzig, 1836.

CRAIG, CLARENCE TUCKER: "Biblical Theology and the Rise of Historicism," *JBL,* 62 (1943), 281-294.

DAVEY, F. N.: "Biblical Theology," *Theo,* 38 (1939), 166-176.

DAVIDSON, ANDREW BRUCE: "Biblical Theology," *Biblical and Literary Essays.* London, 1902.

————— *The Theology of the Old Testament,* ed. by S. D. F. Salmond. Edinburgh, 1904.

DELITZSCH, FRANZ: *Die biblisch-prophetische Theologie, ihre Fortbildung durch Crusius und ihre neuste Entwickelung.* Leipzig, 1845.

DENTAN, ROBERT C.: "The Old Testament and a Theology for Today," *ATR,* 27 (1945), 17-27.

————— "The Nature and Function of Old Testament Theology," *JBR,* 14 (1946), 16-21.

————— "An Exposition of an Old Testament Passage," *JBR,* 15 (1947), 158-161.

DE WETTE, WILHELM MARTIN LEBERECHT: *Biblische Dogmatik des Alten und Neuen Testaments, oder kritische Darstellung der Religionslehre des Hebräismus, des Judenthums und des Urchristenthums.* Berlin, 1813.

DILLMANN, AUGUST: *Handbuch der alttestamentlichen Theologie,* ed. by R. Kittel. Leipzig, 1895.

DUFF, ARCHIBALD: *Old Testament Theology.* London and Edinburgh, 1891.

————— *The Theology and Ethics of the Hebrews.* New York, 1902.

————— *Hints on Old Testament Theology.* London, 1908.

DUHM, BERNHARD: *Die Theologie der Propheten als Grundlage für die innre Entwickelungsgeschichte der Israelitischen Religion.* Bonn, 1875.

EICHRODT, WALTHER: "Hat die alttestamentliche Theologie noch selbständige Bedeutung innerhalb der alttestamentlichen Wissenschaft?" *ZAW,* 47 (1929), 83-91.

———— *Theologie des Alten Testaments.* Vol. 1, *Gott und Volk,* Leipzig, 1933; Vol. 2, *Gott und Welt,* 1935; Vol. 3, *Gott und Mensch,* 1939. Eng. trans. Vol. 1 by J. A. Baker, *Theology of the Old Testament.* London, 1961. Review article by N. K. Gottwald, *ET,* 74 (1963), 209-212.

———— *Das Menschenverständnis des Alten Testaments.* Zurich, 1947. Eng. trans. by K. and R. Gregor Smith, *Man in the Old Testament.* Chicago, 1951.

EISSFELDT, OTTO: "Israelitisch-jüdische Religionsgeschichte und alttestamentliche Theologie," *ZAW,* 44 (1926), 1-12. Reprinted in *Kleine Schriften,* Vol. 1 (Tübingen, 1962), 105-114.

EWALD, HEINRICH: *Die Lehre der Bibel von Gott oder Theologie des Alten und Neuen Bundes.* Leipzig, 1871-76. Eng. trans. by T. Goadby: *Revelation, Its Nature and Record* (Edinburgh, 1884); *Old and New Testament Theology* (Edinburgh, 1888).

FILSON, FLOYD V.: "A New Testament Student's Approach to Biblical Theology," *JBR,* 14 (1946), 22-28.

FOSDICK, HARRY EMERSON: *A Guide to Understanding the Bible: The Development of Ideas within the Old and New Testaments.* New York, 1938.

FOSTER, ROBERT VERRELL: *Old Testament Studies: An Outline of Old Testament Theology.* New York, 1890.

FRITSCH, CHARLES T.: "New Trends in Old Testament Theology," *Bibliotheca Sacra,* 103 (1946), 293-305.

GELIN, ALBERT: *Les idées maîtresses de l'Ancien Testament.* Paris, 1947. Eng. trans. by G. Lamb, *The Key Concepts of the Old Testament.* New York, 1955.

GIRDLESTONE, R. B.: *Old Testament Theology and Modern Ideas.* London, 1909.

GRAMBERG, CARL PETER WILHELM: *Kritische Geschichte der Religionsideen des Alten Testaments.* Berlin, 1829-30.

GRAU, D. R. F.: *Gottes Volk und sein Gesetz: Bruchstücke einer biblischen Theologie des Alten Testaments,* ed. by D. Zöckler. Gütersloh, 1894.

HÄNEL, JOHANNES: *Die Religion der Heiligkeit.* Gütersloh, 1931.

HÄVERNICK, HEINRICH ANDREAS: *Vorlesungen über die Theologie des Alten Testaments,* ed. by E. Hahn. Erlangen, 1848.

HEBERT, ARTHUR GABRIEL: *The Throne of David.* New York, 1941.

—— *The Authority of the Old Testament.* London, 1947.

HEINISCH, PAUL: *Theologie des Alten Testaments.* Bonn, 1940. Eng. trans. by W. Heidt. Collegeville (Minn.), 1950.

HEMPEL, JOHANNES: *Gebet und Frömmigkeit im Alten Testament.* Göttingen, 1922.

—— *Gott und Mensch im Alten Testament.* Stuttgart, 1926.

—— *Das Ethos des Alten Testaments.* Berlin, 1938.

HENGSTENBERG, ERNST WILHELM: *Christologie des Alten Testaments.* Berlin, 1829-35. Eng. trans. by R. Keith. Alexandria, 1836.

HETZENAUER, MICHAEL: *Theologia Biblica.* Vol. 1, *Vetus Testamentum.* Freiburg i. B., 1908.

HITZIG, FERDINAND: *Vorlesungen über die biblische Theologie und messianische Weissagungen des Alten Testaments,* ed. by J. J. Kneucker. Karlsruhe, 1880.

HOFMANN, JOHANN CHRISTIAN KONRAD: *Weissagung und Erfüllung im Alten und Neuen Testamente.* Nördlingen, 1841-44.

—— *Der Schriftbeweis.* Nördlingen, 1852-56.

—— *Biblische Hermeneutik.* Nördlingen, 1880. Eng. trans. by C. Preuss, *Interpreting the Bible.* Minneapolis, 1959.

HYATT, J. PHILIP: *Prophetic Religion.* Nashville, 1947.

IRWIN, WILLIAM A.: "The Reviving Theology of the Old Testament," *JR,* 25 (1945), 235-246.

KAISER, GOTTLIEB PHILIPP CHRISTIAN: *Die biblische Theologie oder Judaismus und Christianismus nach der grammatisch-historischen Interpretationsmethode und nach einer freimütigen Stellung in die kritisch-vergleichende Universalgeschichte der Religionen und in die universale Religion.* Erlangen: Vol. 1, 1813; Vol. 2, 1814; Vol. 3, 1821.

KAUTZSCH, EMIL FRIEDRICH: "The Religion of Israel," *Dictionary of the Bible* (J. Hastings, ed.), extra vol. (1904), 612-734. German trans., *Biblische Theologie des Alten Testaments.* Tübingen, 1911.

KAYSER, AUGUST: *Die Theologie des Alten Testaments in ihrer geschichtlichen Entwickelung dargestellt,* ed. by E. Reuss. Strassburg, 1886. 2nd ed., ed. and rev. by K. Marti. Strassburg, 1894. Retitled *Geschichte der Israelitischen Religion.* Strassburg, 1903.

KITTEL, RUDOLPH: "Die Zukunft der alttestamentlichen Wissenschaft," *ZAW,* 39 (1921), 84-99.

———— *Die Religion des Volkes Israel.* Leipzig, 1921. Eng. trans. by R. C. Micklem, *The Religion of the People of Israel.* New York, 1925.

KNAPP, GEORG CHRISTIAN: *Biblische Glaubenslehre.* Halle, 1840.

KNUDSON, ALBERT C.: *The Religious Teaching of the Old Testament.* New York, 1918.

KOEHLER, LUDWIG: *Theologie des Alten Testaments.* Tübingen, 1936. Eng. trans. by A. S. Todd, *Old Testament Theology.* London, 1957.

KÖNIG, EDUARD: *Geschichte der alttestamentlichen Religion.* Gütersloh, 1915.

———— *Theologie des Alten Testaments kritisch und vergleichend dargestellt.* Stuttgart, 1922.

KUENEN, ABRAHAM: *De Godsdienst van Israel tot den Ondergang van der Joodschen Staat.* Haarlem, 1869. Eng. trans. by A. H. May, *The Religion of Israel to the Downfall of the Jewish State.* London and Edinburgh, 1882.

LINDBLOM, J.: "Zur Frage der Eigenart der alttestamentliche Religion," *Werden und Wesen des Alten Testaments* (J. Hempel et al, eds.; Beiheft 66, *ZAW*). Berlin, 1936; 128-137.

LOFTHOUSE, W. F.: "The Old Testament and Christianity," *Record and Revelation* (H. W. Robinson, ed.). Oxford, 1938; 458-480.

LUTZ, J. L. SAMUEL: *Biblische Dogmatik.* Pforzheim, 1847.

MOELLER, WILHELM and HANS: *Biblische Theologie des Alten Testaments.* Zurich, 1938 (?).

MUILENBURG, JAMES D.: "The Return to Old Testament Theology," *Christianity and the Contemporary Scene* (R. C. Miller and H. H. Shires, eds.). New York, 1943; 30-44.

NOACK, LUDWIG: *Die biblische Theologie des Alten und Neuen Testaments.* Halle, 1853.

NORTH, CHRISTOPHER R.: "The Redeemer God: The Historical Basis of Biblical Theology," *Int,* 2 (1948), 3-16.

———— "Old Testament Theology and the History of Hebrew Religion," *SJT,* 2 (1949), 113-126.

OEHLER, GUSTAV FRIEDRICH: *Prolegomena zur Theologie des Alten Testaments.* Stuttgart, 1845.

———— *Theologie des Alten Testaments.* Tübingen, 1873. Eng. translations: E. D. Smith and S. Taylor, Edinburgh, 1874-75; G. E. Day, *Old Testament Theology,* New York, 1883.

PEDERSEN, JOHS: *Israel, Its Life and Culture*. Copenhagen: Vols. 1-2, 1926; Vols. 3-4, 1940.

PHILLIPS, GODFREY E.: *The Old Testament in the World Church*. London, 1944.

PHYTHIAN-ADAMS, W. J. T.: *The Call of Israel*. Oxford, 1934.

─── *The Fullness of Israel*. Oxford, 1938.

─── "The Foundations of Biblical Theology," *CQR*, 135 (1942), 1-42.

─── *The People and the Presence*. Oxford, 1942.

─── "Shadow and Substance: The Meaning of Sacred History," *Int*, 1 (1947), 419-435.

PIEPENBRING, CHARLES: *Théologie de l'Ancien Testament*. Paris, 1886. Eng. trans. by H. G. Mitchell. New York, 1893.

PORTEOUS, NORMAN W.: "Towards a Theology of the Old Testament," *SJT*, 1 (1948), 136-149.

PORTER, FRANK CHAMBERLAIN: "Crucial Problems in Biblical Theology," *JR*, 1 (1921), 78-81.

─── "Toward a Biblical Theology for the Present," *Contemporary American Theology* (V. Ferm, ed.). New York, 1933; 197-244.

RAD, GERHARD VON: "Das theologische Problem des alttestamentliche Schöpfungsglauben," *Werden und Wesen des Alten Testaments* (J. Hempel et al, eds.; Beiheft 66, *ZAW*). Berlin, 1936; 138-147.

─── "Das formgeschichtliche Problem des Hexateuch," *Beiträge zur Wissenschaft vom Alten und Neuen Testament,* 4 Folge, Heft 26 (Stuttgart, 1938). (Both the above reprinted in G. von Rad, *Gesammelte Studien zum Alten Testament*. Munich, 1958; 136-147, 9-86.)

─── "Grundprobleme einer biblischen Theologie des Alten Testaments," *TL*, 68 (1943), 225-234.

─── "Theologische Geschichtsschreibung im Alten Testament," *TZ*, 4 (1948), 161-174.

RICHARDSON, ALAN: "The Nature of Biblical Theology," *Theo*, 39 (1939), 166-176.

RIEHM, EDUARD: *Alttestamentliche Theologie,* ed. by K. Pahnke. Halle, 1889.

ROBINSON, H. WHEELER: *The Religious Ideas of the Old Testament*. New York, 1913.

————— "The Theology of the Old Testament," *Record and Revelation* (H. W. Robinson, ed.). Oxford, 1938; 303-348.

————— *Inspiration and Revelation in the Old Testament.* Oxford, 1946.

ROST, L.: "Zur Theologie des Alten Testaments: Eine Übersicht," *Christentum und Wissenschaft* (1934), 121 ff.

ROWLEY, H. H.: *The Re-discovery of the Old Testament.* Philadelphia, 1946.

SCHLOTTMANN, KONSTANTIN: *Kompendium der biblischen Theologie des Alten und Neuen Testaments,* ed. by E. Kuhn. Leipzig, 1895.

SCHOLTZ, P.: *Handbuch der Theologie des Alten Bundes im Lichte des Neuen.* Regensburg, 1862.

SCHULTZ, HERMANN: *Alttestamentliche Theologie. Die Offenbarungs-religion auf ihrer vorchristlichen Entwickelungsstufe.* 1st ed., Braunschweig, 1869; 2nd ed., 1878; 4th ed., 1889; 5th ed., Göttingen, 1896. Eng. trans. by J. A. Paterson. Edinburgh, 1892.

SCOTT, R. B. Y.: *The Relevance of the Prophets.* New York, 1944.

SELLIN, ERNST: *Alttestamentliche Theologie auf religionsgeschichtlicher Grundlage.* Vol. 1, *Israelitisch-jüdische Religionsgeschichte;* Vol. 2, *Theologie des Alten Testaments.* Leipzig, 1933.

SMART, JAMES D.: "The Death and Rebirth of Old Testament Theology," *JR,* 23 (1943), 1-11, 124-136.

SMEND, RUDOLPH: *Lehrbuch der alttestamentlichen Religionsgeschichte.* Freiburg and Leipzig, 1893.

SNAITH, NORMAN H.: *The Distinctive Ideas of the Old Testament.* London, 1944.

STADE, BERNHARD: "Über die Aufgaben der biblischen Theologie des Alten Testaments," *ZTK,* 3 (1893), 31-51. Reprinted in *Akademische Reden und Abhandlungen.* Giessen, 1907; 77-96.

————— *Biblische Theologie des Alten Testaments.* Tübingen, 1905.

STAERK, WILLY: "Religionsgeschichte und Religionsphilosophie in ihrer Bedeutung für die biblische Theologie des Alten Testaments," *ZTK,* NF 4 (1923), 289-300.

STEUDEL, JOHANN CHRISTIAN FRIEDRICH: *Vorlesungen über die Theologie des Alten Testaments,* ed. by G. F. Oehler. Berlin, 1840.

STEUERNAGEL, CARL: "Alttestamentliche Theologie und alttestamentliche Religionsgeschichte," *ZAW,* Beiheft 41 (*Martifest-schrift*), 1925, 266-273.

STORR, GOTTLIEB CHRISTIAN: *Doctrinae christianae e solis sacris libris repetitae pars theoretica.* Stuttgart, 1793.

VATKE, WILHELM: *Die biblischen Theologie.* (Part 1: "Die Religion des Alten Testaments nach dem kanonischen Büchern entwickelt.") Berlin, 1835.

VISCHER, WILHELM: *Das Christuszeugnis des Alten Testaments.* Vol. 1, *Das Gesetz.* Zurich, 1934. Eng. trans. by A. B. Crabtree, *The Witness of the Old Testament to Christ.* London, 1949. Vol. 2, *Die früheren Propheten.*

VOS, GERHARDUS: *Biblical Theology.* Grand Rapids, 1948.

WEISER, ARTUR: "Glaube und Geschichte im Alten Testament," *Beiträge zur Wissenschaft vom Alten und Neuen Testament,* 4 Folge, Heft 4 (Stuttgart, 1931).

———— "Die theologische Aufgabe der alttestamentlichen Wissenschaft," *Werden und Wesen des Alten Testaments* (J. Hempel et al., eds.; Beiheft 66, *ZAW*). Berlin, 1936; 207-224.

———— "Das theologische Gesamtverständnis des Alten Testaments," *Deutsche Theologie* (1943), 50-70.

———— "Vom Verstehen des Alten Testaments," *ZAW,* 61 (1945), 17-30. (All the above articles reprinted in A. Weiser, *Glaube und Geschichte im Alten Testament.* Göttingen, 1961.)

WELLHAUSEN, JULIUS: *Geschichte Israels.* Berlin, 1878. Re-titled *Prolegomena zur Geschichte Israels* (1883).

WOLFE, ROLAND E.: "The Terminology of Biblical Theology," *JBR,* 15 (1947), 143-147.

WRIGHT, G. ERNEST: *The Challenge of Israel's Faith.* Chicago, 1944.

ZSCHOKKE, HERMANN: *Theologie der Propheten des Alten Testaments.* Freiburg i. B., 1877.

C. Old Testament Theology 1949-1963

The following list has been made as comprehensive as possible with respect to the subject matter of the foregoing essay—i.e., the history, nature, and method of Old Testament theology, and of "biblical" theology insofar as it is concerned with the Old Testament as well as the New. Attention is also given to literature dealing with such closely related matters as hermeneutics, the authority of Scripture, and the unity of the Testaments. For more wide-ranging discussions of biblical theology in general and for articles and monographs on the subdivisions of Old Testament theology (Doctrine of God, Man, Eschatology, Messianism, etc.) exhaustive bibliographies will be found in the *Internationale Zeitschriftenschau für Bibelwissenschaft und Grenzgebiete* (Düsseldorf, 1951 —) and the "Elenchus bibliographicus" of the journal *Biblica* (Rome, 1920 —). There are also useful bibliographies at the end of chapters in E. Jacob, *Theology of the Old Testament*.

For works published both in Great Britain and the United States, the following list normally gives only a single date and place, ordinarily that of the original publication.

Where titles have been derived from mention in other published works, the reference has usually been checked both for relevance and accuracy. In a few instances this has not been possible and the reference has been included, of necessity, on the strength of the citation alone.

ACHTEMEIER, P. J. and E.: *The Old Testament Roots of Our Faith.* Nashville, 1962.

ACKROYD, P. R.: see KNIGHT, GEORGE A. F.

ALBRIGHT, W. F.: "Return to Biblical Theology," *Christian Century,* 75 (1958), 1328-1331.

ALLEN, E. L.: "The Limits of Biblical Theology," *JBR,* 25 (1957), 13-18.

ALLMEN, J. J. VON (ed.): *Vocabulaire biblique.* Neuchâtel, 1954. Eng. trans. by P. J. Allcock et al., *A Companion to the Bible.* London, 1958.

ANDERSON, B. W. (Ed.): *The Old Testament and Christian Faith.* New York, 1963.

ANDERSON, G. W.: see VRIEZEN, TH. C.

BAAB, OTTO J.: *The Theology of the Old Testament.* Nashville, 1949.

BAKER, J.: "The Construction of an Old Testament Theology," *Theo,* 58 (1955), 252-257.

BARNETT, T. A. M.: "Trends in Old Testament Theology," *CJT,* 6 (1960), 91-101.

BARR, JAMES: "The Problem of Old Testament Theology and the History of Religion," *CJT,* 3 (1957), 141-149.

—— *The Semantics of Biblical Language.* Oxford, 1961.

—— *Biblical Words for Time.* Naperville, 1962.

—— "Hypostatization of Linguistic Phenomena in Modern Theological Interpretation," Journal of Semitic Studies, 7 (1962), 85-94.

—— "Revelation through History in the Old Testament and in Modern Theology," *Int,* 17 (1963), 193-205.

—— See also RAD, GERHARD VON (*Theologie des A.T.*).

BAUER, J. (Ed.): *Bibeltheologisches Wörterbuch.* Graz, 1959.

BAUMGÄRTEL, FRIEDRICH: "Erwägungen zur Darstellung der Theologie des Alten Testaments," *TL,* 76 (1951), 257-272.

—— *Verheissung: zum Frage des evangelischen Verständnisses des Alten Testaments.* Gütersloh, 1952.

—— "Das alttestamentliche Geschehen als 'heilsgeschichtliches' Geschehen," *Geschichte und Alte Testament* (Festschrift for A. Alt). Tübingen, 1953; 13-28.

—— "Das Hermeneutische Problem des Alten Testaments," *TL,* 79 (1954), Sp. 199-212. Reprinted in C. Westermann, *Probleme alttestamentlicher Hermeneutik* (q.v.), 114-139.

BETZ, OTTO: "Biblical Theology, History of," *Interpreter's Dictionary of the Bible* (Nashville, 1962), Vol. A-D, 432-437.

BOMAN, THORLEIF: *Das Hebräische Denken im Vergleich mit dem Griechischen.* Göttingen, 1954. Eng. trans. by J. Moreau, *Hebrew Thought Compared with Greek.* Philadelphia, 1960.

BOUYER, LOUIS: *La Bible et l'Evangile.* Paris, 1951. Eng. trans. by M. P. Ryan, *The Meaning of Sacred Scripture.* Notre Dame, 1958.

BRANTON, J. R.; BROWN, R. A.; BURROWS, M.; and SMART, J. D.: "Our Present Situation in Biblical Theology" (symposium), *RL,* 26 (1956-57), 5-39.

BRIGHT, JOHN: see JACOB, EDMOND.

BROWN, R. A.: see BRANTON, J. R.

BUBER, MARTIN: *The Prophetic Faith.* New York, 1949.

BURROWS, MILLAR: see BRANTON, J. R.

CWIEKOWSKI, FREDERICK J.: "Biblical Theology as Historical Theology," *CBQ,* 24 (1962), 404-410.

DENTAN, ROBERT C.: "The Unity of the Old Testament," *Int,* 5 (1951), 153-173.

—— "Typology, Its Use and Abuse," *ATR,* 34 (1952), 211-217.

————— "The Religion and Theology of the Old Testament," *Encyclopedia Americana* (New York, 1953), Vol. 3, 638-646.

————— *The Design of the Scriptures: A First Reader in Biblical Theology.* New York, 1961.

DUFOUR, X. L. et. al. (Eds.): *Vocabulaire de théologie biblique.* Paris, 1962.

EBELING, GERHARD: "The Meaning of Biblical Theology," *JTS,* NS 6 (1955), 210-225.

————— "Wort Gottes und Hermeneutik," *ZTK,* 56 (1959), 224-251.

EICHRODT, WALTHER: "Ist die typologischer Exegese sachgemässe Exegese?" *TL,* 11 (1956), Sp. 641-654. Reprinted in C. Westermann, *Probleme alttestamentlicher Hermeneutik* (q.v.), 205-226.

————— "Heilserfahrung und Zeitverständnis im Alten Testament," *TZ,* 12 (1956), 103-125.

————— *Das Gottesbild des Alten Testaments.* Stuttgart, 1956.

FERRÉ, NILS F.: "Living Light and Dedicated Decision: Comments on the Relation between Biblical and Systematic Theology," *Int,* 6 (1952), 1-16.

————— "Note by a Theologian on Biblical Hermeneutics," *JBL,* 78 (1959), 105-114. See also under TEEPLE, H. M.

FILSON, FLOYD V.: "Method in Studying Biblical History," *JBL,* 69 (1950), 1-18.

————— "Biblische Theologie in Amerika," *TL,* 75 (1950), 71 ff.

————— "The Unity of the Old and the New Testaments: A Bibliographical Survey," *Int,* 5 (1951), 134-152.

GAMBLE, CONNOLLY JR.: "The Nature of Biblical Theology" (bibliographical survey), *Int,* 5 (1951), 462-467.

————— "The Method of Biblical Theology" (bibliographical survey), *Int,* 9 (1955), 91-99.

GELIN, ALBERT: *L'ame d'Israël dans l'Livre.* Paris, 1957. Eng. trans. by J. R. Foster, *The Religion of Israel* (20th Cent. Enc. of Catholicism). New York, 1959.

————— *Les idées maîtresses de l'Ancien Testament.* Paris, 1947. Trans. by G. Lamb, *The Key Concepts of the Old Testament.* New York, 1955.

GILKEY, L.: "Cosmology, Ontology and the Travail of Biblical Language," *JR,* 41 (1961), 194-205.

GROSS, HEINRICH: "Was ist alttestamentliche Theologie?" *Theologische Zeitschrift* (Trier), 67 (1958), 355-363.

GOTTWALD, N. K.: See under EICHRODT, W.

GUILLET, JACQUES: *Thèmes biblique.* Paris, 1950. Eng. trans., *Themes of the Bible.* Notre Dame, 1960.

HAHN, HERBERT F.: *Old Testament in Modern Research* (chap. 7, "The Theological Approach to the Old Testament"). Philadelphia, 1954.

HEBERT, ARTHUR GABRIEL: *The Bible from Within.* Oxford, 1950. Rev. ed.: *The Old Testament from Within.* Oxford, 1962.

HEMPEL, JOHANNES: "Biblische Theologie und biblische Religionsgeschichte. I. AT," *Die Religion in Geschichte und Gegenwart.* 3rd ed., 1957. Vol. 1, cols. 1256-1259.

―――― "Alttestamentliche Theologie in Protestantischer Sicht heute," *Bibliotheca Orientalis,* 15 (1958), 206-214.

HERBERG, WILL: "Faith as Heilsgeschichte: The Meaning of Redemptive History in Human Existence," *The Christian Scholar,* 39 (1956), 25-31.

HERBERT, ARTHUR S.: "Is There a Theology of the Old Testament?" *ET,* 12 (1950), 361-363.

HERTZBERG, H. W.: *Beiträge zur Traditionsgeschichte und Theologie des Alten Testaments.* Göttingen, 1962.

HESCHEL, ABRAHAM J.: *Theology of Ancient Judaism* (Heb.). London and New York, 1962.

―――― *The Prophets* (chaps. 9-17 on prophetic theology). New York, 1962.

HESSE, F.: "Die Erforschung der Geschichte Israels als theologische Aufgabe," *KD,* 4 (1958), 1-20.

HICKS, R. LANSING: "Present-Day Trends in Biblical Theology," *ATR,* 32 (1950), 136-153.

HIGGINS, A. J. B.: *The Christian Significance of the Old Testament.* London, 1949.

HOFMANN, JOHANN CHRISTIAN KONRAD: see PREUSS, CHRISTIAN.

IMSCHOOT, P.: *Théologie de l'Ancien Testament.* Vol. 1, *Dieu;* Vol. 2, *L'homme;* Vol. 3, . . . Tournai, 1954, 1956, . . .

IRWIN, WILLIAM A.: "Trends in Old Testament Theology," *JBR,* 19 (1951), 183-190.

―――― *The Old Testament, Keystone of Human Culture.* New York, 1952. Expanded from essay "The Hebrews" in H. Frankfort et al. (eds.), *The Intellectual Adventure of Ancient Man.* Chicago, 1946.

―――― "The Interpretation of the Old Testament," *ZAW,* 60 (1952), 1-10.

———— "The Study of Israelite Religion," *VT*, 7 (1957), 111-126.

———— "A Still Small Voice . . . Said, What Are You Doing Here?," *JBL*, 78 (1959), 1-12.

JACOB, EDMOND: *Théologie de l'Ancien Testament*. Neuchâtel, 1955. Eng. trans. by A. W. Heathcote and P. J. Allcock, *Theology of the Old Testament*. London, 1958. Review art. by J. Bright, *ET*, 73 (1962), 304-307.

JEPSEN, A.: "Die Botschaft des Alten Testaments: Überlegungen zum Aufbau einer alttestamentliche Theologie," *Dienst unter dem Wort* (Festschrift for H. Schreiner). Gütersloh, 1953; 149-163.

KING, WINSTON L.: "Some Ambiguities in Biblical Theology," *RL*, 27 (1958), 95-104.

KITTEL, GERHARD, and FRIEDRICH, GERHARD (eds.): *Theologisches Wörterbuch zum Neuen Testament*. Stuttgart, 1933————. Eng. trans. of various arts. have appeared under the title *Bible Key Words*. London and New York, 1949————. The following have thus far been published: "Love," "The Church," "Sin," "Righteousness," "Gnosis," "Apostleship," "Basileia," "Lord," "Spirit of God," "Faith," and "Law."

KNIGHT, GEORGE A. F.: *A Christian Theology of the Old Testament*. London, 1959. Review art. by P. R. Ackroyd, *ET*, 73 (1962), 164-168.

———— *A Biblical Approach to the Doctrine of the Trinity*. SJT Occasional Papers No. 1, 1953.

KOEHLER, LUDWIG: "Christus im Alten und Neuen Testament," *TZ*, 9 (1953).

KRAELING, EMIL G.: *The Old Testament Since the Reformation* (chap. 17, "Toward a Biblical Theology?"). London, 1955.

LACHEMAN, E. R.: "The Renaissance of Biblical Theology" (review art. on the 1st ed. of this book), *JBR*, 19 (1951), 71-75.

LÁKATOS, EUGENIO: "Por una Teología Bíblica basada en los hechos," *Revista Bíblica*, 21 (1959), 83-86, 142-144, 197-200.

LAUER, QUENTIN: "The Genius of Biblical Thought," *The Bridge* (J. M. Oesterreicher, ed.), Vol. 2. New York, 1956; 191-211.

LEARY, A. P.: "Biblical Theology and History," *CQR*, 157 (1956), 402-414.

MACKENZIE, R. A. F.: "The Concept of Biblical Theology," *Catholic Theological Society of America: Proceedings*, 10 (1955), 48-73.

———— *Faith and History in the Old Testament.* Minneapolis, 1963.

MARTIN-ACHARD, ROBERT: "Les voies de la théologie de l'Ancien Testament," *Revue de Théologie et de Philosophie,* 9 (1959), 217-226.

MATHERS, DONALD: "Biblical and Systematic Theology," *CJT,* 5 (1959), 15-24.

McCASLAND, S. VERNON: "The Unity of the Scriptures," *JBL,* 73 (1954), 1-10.

McKENZIE, JOHN L.: "Problems of Hermeneutics in Roman Catholic Exegesis," *JBL,* 77 (1958), 197-204.

———— "The Task of Biblical Theology," *The Voice of St. Mary's Seminary,* 36 (1959), 7-9, 26-27.

MICHAELI, FRANK: "Grammaire hébraïque et théologie biblique," *Hommage à Wilhelm Vischer* (Montpellier, 1960), 145-156.

MOWINCKEL, SIGMUND: *Det Gamle Testament som Guds Ord.* Oslo, 1938. Eng. trans. by R. B. Bjornard, *The Old Testament as Word of God.* Nashville, 1959.

MUILENBURG, JAMES: "Preface to Hermeneutics," *JBL,* 77 (1958), 18-26.

———— *The Way of Israel.* New York, 1961.

OSTERLOH, E. and ENGELLAND, H. (Eds.): *Biblisch-theologisches Handwörterbuch zum Lutherbibel.* 2nd. rev. ed., Göttingen, 1959.

PAYNE, J. BARTON: *The Theology of the Older Testament.* Grand Rapids, 1962.

PFEIFFER, ROBERT H.: "Fact and Faith in Biblical History," *JBL,* 70 (1951), 1-14.

PIDOUX, GEORGES: *L'homme dans l'Ancien Testament.* Neuchâtel, 1953.

PIPER, OTTO A.: "Biblical Theology and Systematic Theology," *JBR,* 25 (1957), 106-111.

PORTEOUS, NORMAN W.: "Semantics and Old Testament Theology," *Oudtestamentische Studiën,* 8 (1950), 1-14.

———— "Old Testament Theology," *The Old Testament and Modern Study* (H. H. Rowley, ed.). Oxford, 1951; 312-345.

———— "The Old Testament and Some Theological Thought Forms," *SJT,* 7 (1954), 153-169.

———— "The Theology of the Old Testament," *Peake's Commentary on the Bible* (London, 1962), 151-159.

PREUSS, CHRISTIAN: "The Contemporary Relevance of von Hofmann's Hermeneutical Principles," *Int,* 4 (1950), 311-321.

PROCKSCH, OTTO: *Theologie des Alten Testaments.* Gütersloh, 1949.

PRUSSNER, FREDERICK C.: *A Methodology for Old Testament Theology.* Unpub. diss., Univ. of Chicago, 1953.

RAD, GERHARD VON: "Typologische Auslegung des Alten Testaments," *EvT,* 12 (1952-53), 17-34. Reprinted in part, "Das Alte Testament ist ein Geschichtsbuch," *Probleme alttestamentlicher Hermeneutik,* C. Westermann, ed. (q.v.). Eng. trans. by J. Bright, "Typological Interpretation of the Old Testament," *Int,* 15 (1961), 174-192.

———— *Theologie des Alten Testaments.* Vol. 1, *Die Theologie der geschichtlichen Überlieferungen Israels,* Munich, 1957; Vol. 2, *Die Theologie der prophetischen Überlieferungen Israels,* 1960. Eng. trans. by D. M. G. Stalker, *Old Testament Theology.* Vol. 1, Edinburgh, 1962. Review art. by J. Barr, *ET,* 73 (1962), 142-146; also, by W. Zimmerli, *VT,* 13 (1963), 100-111.

REARDON, B. M. G.: "Has 'Biblical Theology' Served its Turn?" *Theo,* 58 (1955), 9-12.

REID, J. K. S.: *The Authority of Scripture.* London, 1957.

RENDTORFF, ROLF: "Hermeneutik des Alten Testaments als Frage nach der Geschichte," *ZTK,* 57 (1960), 27-40.

———— and KOCH, KLAUS (eds.): *Studien zur Theologie der alttestamentlichen Überlieferungen* (Festschrift for G. von Rad). Neukirchen Kreis Moers, 1961.

REVENTLOW, H. GRAF VON: "Grundfrage der alttestamentlichen Theologie im Lichte der neueren deutschen Forschung," *TZ,* 17 (1961), 81-98.

RICHARDSON, ALAN (ed.): *A Theological Word Book of the Bible.* London, 1950.

———— *The Biblical Doctrine of Work.* London, 1952.

———— "Historical Theology and Biblical Theology," *CJT,* 1 (1955), 157-167. See also WERNHAM, J. C. S.

ROWLEY, H. H.: *The Biblical Doctrine of Election.* London, 1950.

———— *The Unity of the Bible.* London, 1953.

———— *The Faith of Israel.* London, 1956.

RULER, ARNOLD A. VAN: *Die Christliche Kirche und das Alte Testament.* Munich, 1955.

RYLAARSDAM, J. COERT: "Preface to Hermeneutics," *JR,* 30 (1950), 79-89.

―――― "The Problem of Faith and History in Biblical Interpretation," *JBL*, 77 (1958), 26-32.

SCHWEITZER, WOLFGANG: "Biblical Theology and Ethics Today," *Biblical Authority for Today* (A. Richardson and W. Schweitzer, eds.). London, 1951.

SIMPSON, CUTHBERT A.: "Old Testament Historiography and Revelation," *HJ*, 56 (1958), 319-332.

―――― "An Inquiry into the Biblical Theology of History," *JTS*, NS 12 (1961), 1-13.

SMART, JAMES D.: see BRANTON, J. R.

―――― *The Interpretation of Scripture*. Philadelphia, 1961.

SMITH, CHARLES RYDER: *The Bible Doctrine of Man*. London, 1951.

―――― *The Bible Doctrine of Sin*. London, 1953.

―――― *The Bible Doctrine of Grace*. London, 1956.

―――― *The Bible Doctrine of the Hereafter*. London, 1958.

SOGGIN, J. ALBERTO: "Alttestamentliche Glaubenszeugnisse und geschichtliche Wirklichkeit," *TZ*, 6 (1961), 385-398.

STENDAHL, KRISTER: "Biblical Theology, Contemporary," *Interpreter's Dictionary of the Bible* (Nashville, 1962), Vol. A-D, 418-432.

STOKES, MACK B.: *The Epic of Revelation: An Essay in Biblical Theology*. New York, 1961.

TEEPLE, HOWARD M.: "Notes on Theologians' Approach to the Bible," *JBL*, 79 (1960), 164-166.

TOOMBS, LAWRENCE E.: "O. T. Theology and the Wisdom Literature," *JBR*, 23 (1955), 193-196.

TRESMONTANT, CLAUDE: *Essai sur la pensée hébraïque*. 2nd ed., Paris, 1956. Eng. trans. by M. F. Gibson, *A Study of Hebrew Thought*. New York, 1960.

VAUX, ROLAND DE: "A propos de la théologie biblique," *ZAW*, 68 (1956), 225-227.

VICARY, D. R.: "Liberalism, Biblical Criticism, and Biblical Theology," *ATR*, 34 (1950), 114-121.

VRIEZEN, TH. C.: *Hoofdlijnen der Theologie van het Oude Testament*. Wageningen, 1954. Eng. trans. by S. Neuijen, *An Outline of Old Testament Theology*. Oxford (Blackwell), 1958. Review art. by G. W. Anderson, *ET*, 73 (1962), 113-116.

WATSON, PHILIP S.: "The Nature and Function of Biblical Theology, *ET*, 73 (1962), 195-200.

WERNBERG-MØLLER, P.: "Is There an Old Testament Theology?" *HJ*, 59 (1960), 21-29.

WERNHAM, JAMES C. S.: "Historical and Biblical Theology: A Reply to Alan Richardson," *CJT*, 2 (1956).

WESTERMANN, CLAUS (ed.): *Probleme alttestamentlicher Hermeneutik*. Munich, 1960. Eng. trans., *Essays on Old Testament Hermeneutics*. Richmond, 1963.

WILDENBERGER, H.: "Auf dem Wege zu einer biblischen Theologie: Erwägungen zur Hermeneutik des Alten Testaments," *EvT*, 19 (1959), 70-90.

WOLFF, HANS WALTER: "Zur Hermeneutik des Alten Testaments," *EvT*, 16 (1956), 337-370. Reprinted in C. Westermann, *Probleme alttestamentlicher Hermeneutik* (q.v.), 140-180. Eng. trans. by K. Crim, "The Hermeneutics of the Old Testament," *Int*, 15 (1961), 439-472.

WRIGHT, G. ERNEST: *The Old Testament against its Environment*. Chicago, 1950.

———— "The Unity of the Bible," *Int*, 5 (1951), 131-133, 304-317.

———— *God Who Acts: Biblical Theology as Recital*. Chicago, 1952.

———— "The Faith of Israel," *Interpreter's Bible* (Nashville, 1952), Vol. 1, 349-389.

———— *The Biblical Doctrine of Man in Society*. London, 1954.

———— "The Unity of the Bible," *SJT*, 8 (1955), 337-352.

———— *The Rule of God: Essays in Biblical Theology*. Garden City, 1960.

YOUNG, EDWARD J.: *The Study of Old Testament Theology Today*. London, 1958.

ZIMMERLI, WALTHER: *Das Menschenbild des Alten Testamentes*. Munich, 1949.

———— "Verheissung und Erfüllung," *EvT*, 12 (1952-53), 34-59. Reprinted in C. Westermann, *Probleme alttestamentlicher Hermeneutik* (q.v.), 69-101.

———— *Das Alte Testament als Anrede*. Munich, 1956.

INDEX OF PROPER NAMES IN TEXT